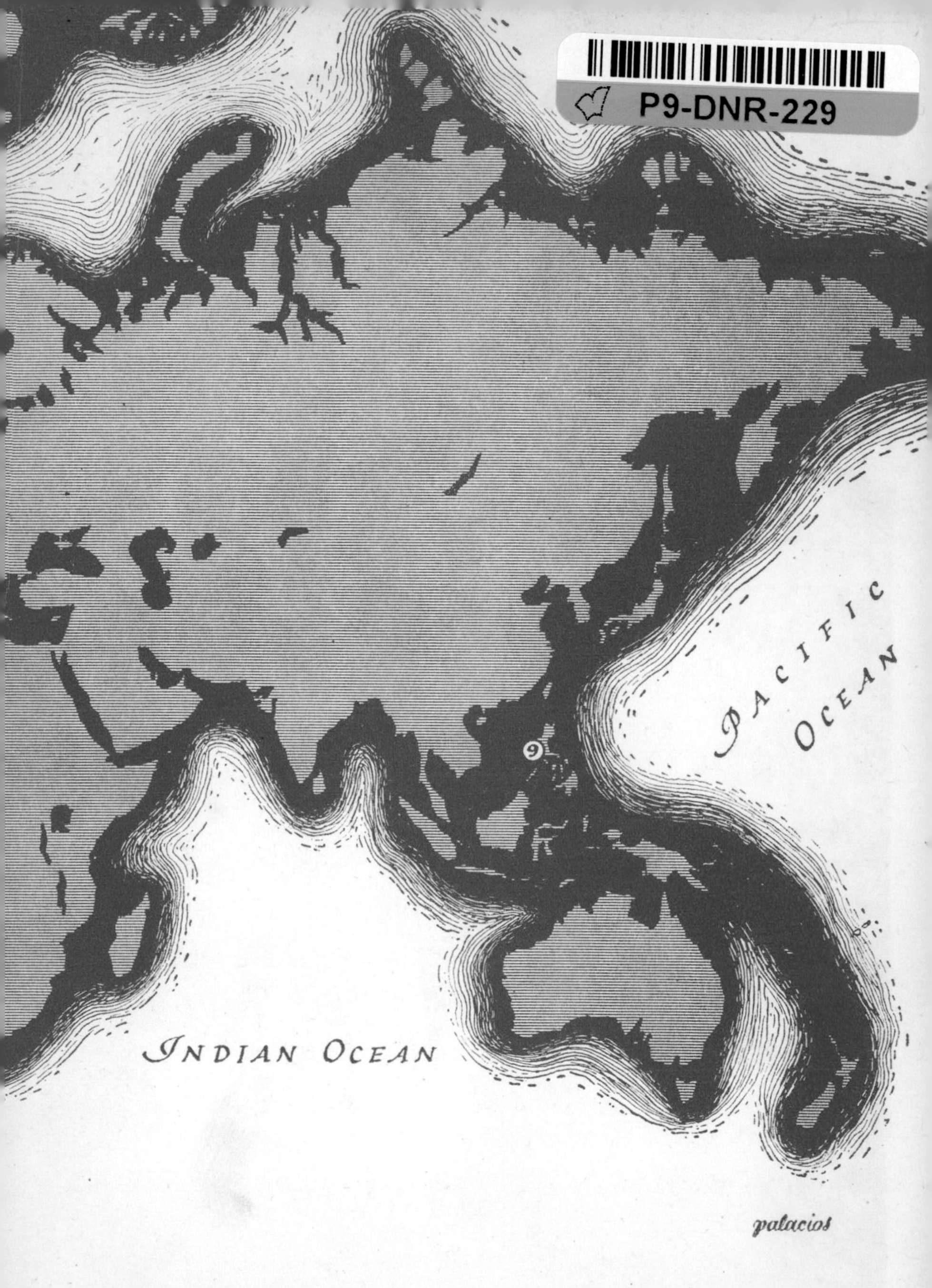

⑩ Fort Lewis, Washington, 1940-41. ⑪ Washington, D.C., 1941-42.
⑫ United Kingdom, 1942. ⑬ North Africa, 1942-43.
⑭ Sicily, Italy, 1943. ⑮ United Kingdom, 1944.
⑯ Normandy and Paris, France, 1944.
⑰ Paris and Versailles, France, 1945. ⑱ Washington, D.C., 1945-48.
⑲ New York City, N.Y., 1948-50. ⑳ Paris, France, 1951.

LIBRARY
EMORY & HENRY
COLLEGE
EMORIUM et HENRICENSE COLLEGIUM
MACTE VIRTUTE
MDCCCXXXVI
EMORY, VIRGINIA
WITHDRAWN

MAN FROM ABILENE

MAN FROM ABILENE

BY KEVIN McCANN
PRESIDENT OF THE DEFIANCE COLLEGE

1952 · DOUBLEDAY & COMPANY, INC., GARDEN CITY, NEW YORK

PRINTED IN THE UNITED STATES
FIRST EDITION

LIBRARY OF CONGRESS CATALOG CARD NUMBER 52-6738

To the men and women of The Defiance College because for me they are assurance that America shall never lack Dwight and Mamie Eisenhowers.

FOREWORD

This book, reluctantly begun, is reluctantly ended. In the summer of 1951 its writing was first proposed to me. I then protested my inability to cover so complex and many-sided a subject as Dwight Eisenhower in the time and space dictated by publishing schedules. However, the publisher's assurance that he sought a survey, not an exhaustive treatise, lessened my protests. Later, a decision that the sales royalties would go to the scholarship fund of The Defiance College silenced them. Money for scholarships catalyzes a college president's hesitation into action.

I began work in August. My original goal was little more than a detailed character sketch. In September I had to put the manuscript aside because, during the first two months of a new school year, a college president is hardly master of his own time. This is particularly true of a freshman president. When I resumed work on the manuscript in November, I broadened the scope of my objective. Now that I am finished, I am not sure that I have approached, much less hit, my mark.

My revised purpose has been neither outright biography nor analytical dissection of Dwight Eisenhower's philosophy. The former has been done well by Kenneth Davis. No new account of dates and anecdotes is needed. A philosophical study, on the other hand, is not feasible until the passage of years permits sharpness of focus and solidness of judgment. At least, in my case, dissection requires an objectivity, a detachment in time and interest, that I cannot hope ever to possess.

Rather, my intent has been a portrait, so to speak, of the thinking Eisenhower against a backdrop of principles, attitudes, hopes, and ideals. By his own words, of course, he has already painted the fullest such portrait. None could hope to improve on it, in accuracy, in depth, in fullness. These qualities are more important, I think, than the labored novelty of a new approach or interpretation. Much of the book, consequently, is Eisenhower's own. Selection of material from letters, random jottings, memoranda, published and unpublished talks has been my principal task. In that light I am a carpenter who has built a framework, not an author who has made a book.

Deliberately I restricted myself to the man himself. Herein he appears largely as a solitary figure, at his desk writing, on the platform speaking, in his room thinking. I have ignored those about him, now and in the past, although in many ways they equal him in color and in many ways reflect facets of his personality. Beyond simplicity of presentation, I had ample warrant for this omission.

If he always has relied much on others, Eisenhower, in all things decisive and critical, has stood apart from them, measuring their counsel against his own convictions. Seldom physically alone, for he is typically American in his gregariousness, he has always seemed curiously independent of those about him. It may be argued that what he has done in the past has been more often done on orders from above or on professional advice from below than on his own initiative; and there is some truth in the argument. But what he has thought has ever been his own work alone. Today, what he has thought and what he thinks are far more important than what he has done or the names and faces of his various staffs. Few men in public life have so frankly revealed their thinking.

Nevertheless, the thinking Eisenhower is not entirely portrayed by his written or spoken words. His physical appearance, his attitude toward the games he plays or the chores he performs are often far more enlightening than his correspondence or his speeches. Yet, had I dwelt on those elements, the resulting portrait would be seen through the glasses of my prejudice. In this election year, certainly, my presentation would be suspect. In fact, even the most objective portrayal of the day-to-day Eisenhower might be suspect, for in a host of ways he seems too good to be true. Yet in most ways he is better than he seems.

MAN FROM ABILENE

CHAPTER ONE

DWIGHT DAVID EISENHOWER is, in all important respects, a simple man who, during the past ten years, has risen to a position of global responsibility without parallel in the history of the world. He stands today at the head of great international military forces, poised to defend the peaceful integrity of Western civilization. For the second time in a single decade he has forged the divergent interests of several nations into a unified force bound to a single goal. More than simply a military hero, however, Eisenhower has emerged in ten short years as one of the great political catalysts of our time—a man whose mere presence seems to overcome national boundaries and the force of whose personality can dissolve the traditional conflicts that for centuries have held the European nations apart.

Yet as recently as 1941, Eisenhower's greatest ambition was simply to command a single American division, while in the years preceding our entry into the Second World War his career was, except for two or three striking differences, not appreciably unlike that of any other senior United States Army officer who, having graduated from West Point before World War I, could anticipate a routine series of assignments and promotions until retirement.

What then accounts for Eisenhower's phenomenal growth as a leader and where in his background are the sources of his tremendous vitality? How does he differ from so many other members of the generation of which he seems to be typical? And why, now that he has risen to a position of world leadership, does he seem so reluctant to play the hero's role?

The answers to these questions are as simple and as complex as the man himself. In many ways they are as vexed as the answers to the questions concerning America's own growth in world leadership during the past fifty years, for in the broadest sense Eisenhower stands as typical not only of his generation but of his country at large. To many parts of the world and particularly to Europe he is himself America, representing precisely those qualities by which our country and its people are known.

Yet when he was born sixty-one years ago, neither he nor his country could fairly have anticipated their future ascendancy, despite the fact that the seeds of their growth were firmly planted and in some places beginning to sprout.

Abilene, Kansas, where Eisenhower lived from his infancy until he was twenty, was a small town only a few decades from the frontier. The lusty pioneer energies that built it had moved farther West, but they left behind a robust, independent settlement whose rugged population knew the value of hard work and took for granted the virtues of sturdy individualism.

Eisenhower's own family was poor by today's standards. His parents who had come out from the East with a certain amount of capital lost their stake early. Their home, built on a small three-acre plot offered few comforts and instead obliged its occupants to work the surrounding garden from morning till night, for indeed their very lives depended upon it.

Even so Eisenhower's boyhood was typical—in fact it was ordinary. He attended the local schools, worked for a while in a creamery, and formed the usual friendships. Though some of his contemporaries remember him as rather more energetic than most boys, no one could have guessed during his early years what the future held in store for him. To all outward appearances he was simply another boy from Abilene, as uncertain as the next of his place in the world but as determined as any to do the best job he could.

As was true of so many other Midwestern youngsters, his earliest and most enduring influences stemmed from a family environment saturated in faith predicated on the practical conviction that mere good works alone are not enough to assure survival. Eisenhower's own family had come West from Pennsylvania with a sect known as the River Brethren whose dominant characteristics were severe piety and uncompromising pacifism. They founded their community in Abilene largely for the sake of achieving a more direct communion with God, unhindered by a built-up society. And they demanded from their members strict adherence to the principles of their pursuasion.

There is no evidence that Eisenhower either rebelled against the rigidity of this sect or that he accepted its strictures without question. Like most of his contemporaries who found themselves in similar circumstances, he seems simply to have stayed with it until gradually its hold on him lessened and then, almost imperceptibly, he seems to have left it behind and directed his attention to the more urgent demands of the new generation, whose buoyant self-assurance left no room for the narrow sectarianism of earlier years.

When Eisenhower left Abilene for West Point, not only he himself but the entire nation stood on the verge of a new era. The pioneer energies that had surged through the wilderness had overflowed their banks and were spreading rapidly with no apparent direction to all corners of the country, and within a few years they were to spread still farther, making their mark on the Old World as well as on the new one.

Just what these energies were and how they affected the men who seemed to become their masters is still a matter for speculation. We ourselves are too close to them to understand either their origins or their possible consequences. Yet we are in a position, if not to know the heart of the problem, at least to witness its outward manifestations and to see the situation in miniature in the lives of the men who seem to typify it most.

Eisenhower is a symbol of his time and place as few other great men in history have ever been. Through whatever combination of circumstances it has become his responsibility to stand before the world as a symbol of cultural progressivism and as one of its chief, active proponents. He not only embodies to a remarkable degree the characteristics which have come to be classified under the general heading of dynamic Americanism, but he also carries with them an amazing vitality and personal charm which enable him to impart their significance to a world sorely in need of their support. But the question remains: How did these energies originate? And why has Eisenhower—more than any other man—been able to work with them in an area where they have traditionally been regarded with suspicion and hostility.

Eisenhower himself has frequently asserted that any number of his contemporaries are as well qualified as he is himself to assume the responsibilities of leadership. He has never thought of himself as great nor is it likely that he ever anticipated—or even now fully appreciates—the real significance of his role in history. Yet the fact is that Dwight Eisenhower, whose roots are firmly planted in the rich soil of America's Midwest and whose every action reflects the ordinary behavior of his average countryman, has grown to a position of world leadership without parallel in history. And he has risen to this stature almost exactly in proportion as the United States itself has. He is indeed its typical representative of greatness.

CHAPTER TWO

WHETHER EISENHOWER was born with the quality of leadership, whether he achieved it, or whether it was thrust upon him, is far too perplexed a question to admit a simple answer. One finds, however, that until the last days of 1941, when he was called to Washington to serve in the War Plans Division of the War Department and from there appointed Commander in Chief of the European Theater of Operations, there were few tangible evidences of what the future held for him.

During the preceding two years, his career had been almost oppressively commonplace. Like so many other Army officers of his generation he was involved in apparently endless routine activities, and again like so many others he longed for a regimental assignment that would put him in the field with troops. Yet it was during these two years that his career underwent its major transformation, bringing him from public anonymity to supreme command. The transformation developed along the following lines.

From early 1940 until June 1941, he was stationed at Fort Lewis, at the foot of Puget Sound in the state of Washington. At first he served as executive officer for the 15th Infantry regiment and later, in November 1940, he became chief of staff of the Third Division of which the 15th was a part. Five months later, in March 1941, he was appointed chief of staff of the IX Army Corps, with the temporary rank of colonel, only one grade higher than the commission he had held during World War I.

Naturally enough he bridled at his office responsibilities, and though his complaints were generally qualified by good humor, he continued to look forward to a regimental command. For a few short weeks during the summer of 1940, he actually did manage to get into the field, and on August 23 he wrote an exuberant letter to his old friend, Colonel L. T. Gerow, about the brief maneuvers in which he participated.

We've just returned from maneuvers. For four days and nights we attacked through country that is mainly so-called cutover. Actually it would have made a good stage-setting for a play in Hades. Stumps, slashings, fallen logs, tangled brush, holes, hummocks and hills! While I am Regimental Executive, I asked for, and got, command of a battalion—and we certainly went places and did things.

Certain things stood out:

A. *The Infantry Regiment needs more transportation; roughly one more 1½ ton truck per rifle company, two 1½ ton trucks in the Regimental Headquarters Company (in place of ½ tons) and about three more in the Service Company.*

B. *On the other hand the methods of using foot troops and trucks on a single, rather poor road, especially when all other elements of the combat team are following closely, have* not *been perfected.*

C. *In difficult country the battalion communications, particularly when the battalion is allotted a considerable frontage, are inadequate. This was noticed particularly in our maneuvers because of lack of experienced officers. In my battalion, aside from myself, there are two first lieutenants, Regular Army, two second lieutenants, Regular Army, and the rest Tommys. My staff was one Tommy second lieutenant. Maintenance of control is a real job! Mighty close to an impossible one!*

As yet we've received no light machine guns nor BAR*'s 1918-A-2's, nor any 60-mm. Mortars. Finally, the regiment was some four hundred men short of authorized strength.*

In general, that's the alibi side of the picture. For the rest we really learned a lot, shook down our organization and on top of it all, had a lot of fun. I froze at night, never had in any one stretch more than 1¾ hours' sleep, and at times was really fagged out. . . .

In the meantime, while Eisenhower was concerned with the inadequacies of a single United States regiment, the critical situation in Europe was making it more apparent every day that America's military shortcomings were not limited to the absence of a few trucks and rifles. The country was desperately in need of a large army. It had fewer than 300,000 men under arms.

Within a few months, however, Selective Service had swollen the ranks considerably. Through the draft, thousands of recruits arrived each week in the reception centers for classification and assignment to various arms and services; in posts across the country for basic training; in regimental and divisional areas for the unit exercises and final polish that would make them soldiers. In less than a year the United States possessed the largest army in its peacetime history. For every regular officer, skilled in the profession of arms, there was no ceiling to advancement—certainly not if he had caught the eye and had won the approval of Lieutenant General Lesley J. McNair, whose job it was to build a tough combat force of infantry, armor, and artillery.

In August 1940, when McNair came to Fort Lewis, Eisenhower did not catch the visitor's eye. He was away on maneuvers. Later he wrote to Mark Clark, who, at the time, was on McNair's staff:

What you say about General McNair agrees exactly with what I've always heard about him. . . . I am deeply regretful I never had a chance to meet him; but when he visited our C.P. during the recent maneuvers I just couldn't take a minute off; not even if at that moment old Gabriel had blown his trumpet.

It was characteristic of Eisenhower then, as it is now, for him to attend strictly to the business at hand, whatever the personal consequences might be. The trait echoes throughout his entire career, influencing not only his minor decisions but the most important ones he has ever had to make. And because of it, he remained for the time being at his desk in Fort Lewis.

Later, Clark himself visited Fort Lewis on a tour of inspection. Again Eisenhower brought up the subject of a troop command for himself, but to no avail. By the end of October he was still at his desk. On the last day of the month he wrote a long letter to Clark that included the following paragraphs:

I thought I made it clear, in one of my notes to you, that I was quite keen to get a command in the Armored Corps. As you know, George Patton rather expects to get one of the new divisions that are to be organized next year. When he wrote me, he thought such organization would take place in January, but I now hear that it is deferred until June. In any event, that is exactly the thing I would like to do and I am sure that George Patton intends to ask for me in that capacity. The only difficulty that I can anticipate is that the War Department, because of my somewhat junior rank or for some other reason, may turn him down.

In the meantime, I am delighted that they are not going

to yank me out of the 15th Infantry on any excuse whatsoever. In the note to you the other day, I asked you to confirm once more, with the Chief of Infantry, the intention of that office to let me alone, so that I would be available for the armored force when the time comes. In the light of what you tell me now, I see it was unnecessary to make that request of you. However, it is perfectly okay with me if the personnel section in that office is aware of the fact that I have an ambition to command one of the next armored regiments to be formed. They will probably think me a conceited individual, but I see no objection to setting your sights high. Actually, of course, I will be delighted to serve in the Armored Corps in almost any capacity, but I do hope to avoid Staff and to stay on troop duty for some time to come. And since I notice that in the original assignments they gave one of the armored regiments to a lieutenant colonel, I will hope that they might think that much of me also.

But during the following weeks Eisenhower was too busy with staff details to think further of a troop assignment. Then, on November 18, 1940, he received the following radiogram from Gerow who had just become a brigadier general heading the War Plans Division of the War Department General Staff:

I NEED YOU IN WAR PLANS DIVISION DO YOU SERIOUSLY OBJECT TO BEING DETAILED ON THE WAR DEPT GENERAL STAFF AND ASSIGNED HERE PLEASE REPLY IMMEDIATELY

All at once Eisenhower's hopes for a field command seemed on the point of complete destruction. A post in the W.P.D. would inevitably remove him from troops indefinitely and, conceivably, classify him once and for all as a staff officer. Throughout the following day he worried out an answer to Gerow's request. His reply, he knew, would be crucial to his entire career. If he accepted, his chances for a regiment would be effectively ended. If he refused, there was always the possibility that he would stay at Fort Lewis, and remain on the IX Corps staff indefinitely. On November 19, he wrote to Gerow as follows:

Dear Gee:

Your telegram, arriving this morning, sent me into a tailspin. I am going to tell you the whole story and then if you decide that I should come to the War Plans Division, all you have to do is have the orders issued without any further reference to me.

In the first place, I want to make it clear that I am, and have always been, very serious in my belief that the individual's preference and desires should have little, if any weight in determining his assignment, when superior authority is making a decision in the matter. So all the rest of this is because, by implication, you asked for it!

With this somewhat pompous-sounding preamble, here goes.

There is no other individual that ranks with yourself so far as my personal choice of commanders is concerned. You have known this for so many years that it seems redundant to repeat it. I have never been so flattered in my life as by the inclusion, in your telegram, of the word "need" as you used it.

Next, I have, in the few short months I have been allowed to serve with troops, completely reassured myself that I am capable of handling command jobs. I feel confident that my superiors' reports have and will show this, and certainly I have had nothing but the most splendid co-operation and loyalty from those who have served under me. But in this Army, today, such self-confidence (or egotism if you choose to call it that) does not appear to be sufficient when some of the ritualistic-minded people begin to scrutinize the record. They *simply say, "He has had only six months' actual duty with troops since 1922. He cannot possibly be given a regiment or what have you."*

As I wrote you when you were at Benning, I have resisted every suggestion that I leave troops, not so particularly because I felt that after so many years of staff duty I was entitled to my own turn at the more fascinating work of handling soldiers, but also in conformity with the War Department policy that requires a certain proportion of troop duty in order for a man to be considered a capable and rounded officer. In correspondence with friends in Washington, I have consistently indicated my desire to stay with troops, either with the 15th, or, if possible, in command of one of the mechanized units to be organized in the spring.

At various times I have had informal reports from Wash-

ington, to the effect that I had been requested for positions on certain corps and division staffs. My informants have told me that in each such instance the War Department (Chief of Infantry) has declined to give favorable consideration, on the ground that I needed duty with troops. In one instance, where I am told a corps commander (I believed to be General Krueger) asked for me as his chief of staff, the answer was that I was too junior in rank for that post.

I suppose that you have informally investigated the attitude of the Chief of Infantry and the Adjutant General, or possibly even of the Chief of Staff, toward assigning me to the W.D.G.S. and are, therefore, sure that if you put in the request it will be approved. Incidentally, another question interjects itself and that is the one concerning the provisions of law affecting eligibility for the General Staff! Naturally, if a fellow is going to serve in a General Staff position, he would like to get official credit for doing so, and unless the Department has waived normal eligibility rules for the period of the emergency, it might be impossible to have me assigned. Again, however, I presume that you have investigated this particular point.

All the above seems to be a lot of beating the devil around the bush. However, it is almost necessary to recite these things to you so that you can understand the reasons for the somewhat confused state of mind in which I now find myself. Oh yes! another thing I should probably tell you is that General Thompson is merely awaiting favorable action on a recommendation of his, regarding a new assignment for his present division chief of staff, before putting my name before the War Department to fill that position. I believe, however, that that particular request has not yet gone forward, as I am sure he is awaiting the result of his first recommendation.

To summarize, then, my ideas on the matter:

For both Mamie and me the thought of renewing our old close companionship with you is a delightful prospect.

From the official angle, assuming that all the obvious objections to my present assignment to the General Staff have been eliminated, I would like, before the matter is officially consummated, for those in authority to know that I have earnestly tried for many years to get an assignment to troops and to serve at least a normal tour with them. Unfortunately, General MacArthur would never allow those requests to be made of record. I know that General Marshall, in person, is not concerned with the assignment of such small fry as myself; but I would like to see the matter so handled that not only is the attention of the Chief of Infantry and the Adjutant General, but if possible, even that of the Chief of Staff attracted to the above facts. Particularly, I would like to see it clearly noted in the official records. I think it's just a matter of pride, but I don't want to be considered, on the basis of records, as unfit *for duty with troops.*

But, if you're satisfied that the matter is understood by all, as I've roughly indicated, go ahead!

Finally, if I am ordered to Washington, I would like to have the orders framed, if possible, so as to order me and my household goods there by rail. This would allow me to make a short visit with both Mamie's and my family on the way to my new station. I would need, of course, about ten days' leave on the way.

I hope that all of this does not sound too demanding or unreasonable. I do not need to tell you that whatever I am told to do will be done as well as I know how to do it, but since your radio seemed to request my complete reactions to your suggestion, I have tried to put them before you fully and frankly. Please send me advance notice, by radio, of the final decision.

P. S. *By the way, if you are living in an apartment house in Washington, would there be any chance for Mamie and me to get into the same building? And if war starts, I expect to see you raise the roof to get a command, and I go along!*

On the morning of November 23, Eisenhower received Gerow's reply:

AFTER CAREFUL CONSIDERATION OF CONTENTS OF YOUR LETTER AND THE WISHES OF GENERAL THOMPSON AS INDICATED TO G1 I HAVE WITHDRAWN MY REQUEST FOR YOUR DETAIL TO WAR PLANS DIVN WILL WRITE DETAILS LATER REGRET OUR SERVICE TOGETHER MUST BE POSTPONED

Two days later, when Eisenhower answered Gerow, thanking him for his consideration, the matter was effectively ended. But once again he referred regretfully to his sedentary assignment, as well as to other matters of a more personal but nonetheless painful nature.

For the past two weeks I've been suffering with the "shingles." Don't laugh; it's one of the most painful things you ever heard of. The doctors tried to put me to bed, but I found I was less miserable with something to occupy my time and mind, and so have kept going. I think I'm over the worst of it now—and I most certainly don't want the disease again. . . .

I don't suppose I've told you that for the past six weeks I've been serving as General Thompson's "executive." He was getting snowed under with his division and with the additional job of reorganizing command and administrative systems, to say nothing of facilities for an eventual garrison of some forty-five thousand men. So, "in addition to other duties" I was assigned as executive, to serve as such until a Regular officer should be assigned here to the post complement. . . .

Actually, Gee, the job of staying with a regiment is a damn near hopeless one. I landed at San Francisco on January 6, hurrying to join the 15th before it sailed for Monterey on landing exercises. At the dock I was met and told to go to Fourth Army staff for one month—which I did. I then joined the regiment and within a month I was battling to keep from going with the Navy on a two months' cruise. Finally, General DeWitt let me off that and General Sweeney immediately made me the "chief umpire" for all divisional maneuvers at Camp Ord. That took another month. Then two suggestions were made—one that I be deputy chief umpire for the Fourth Army Maneuvers, in August, the other that I be President of Rents and Claims Board for the same operation. I talked myself out of both those. Then, at the end of September, I was put on this job! So there you are. I've enjoyed the regimental "intervals," particularly the Fourth Army Maneuvers, where I had my own battalion.

Meanwhile Krueger's search for a staff to direct his Third Army was nearing its conclusion. Mark Clark, who was conducting the search on his behalf, had just returned from a 60,000 mile tour of the country looking for the best officers in the service. By June 1941, he had made his choice. Eisenhower, who had held out against Gerow for a regiment of his own, received the following orders:

June 24, 1941: "Colonel Dwight D. Eisenhower (O-3822), General Staff Corps, is relieved from assignment and duty at headquarters, IX Army Corps, Fort Lewis, Washington, is assigned to headquarters, Third Army, San Antonio, Texas, and will proceed to that station and report to the commanding general, Third Army, for duty with the General Staff Corps." The crucial phase of his transformation from just another United States Army officer had begun.

A week later he received these further orders:

July 2, 1941: "Colonel Dwight D. Eisenhower (O-3822), General Staff Corps, having reported at this headquarters in compliance with paragraph 4, Special Orders No. 146, War Department, C. S., is announced as deputy chief of staff, Third Army."

Krueger had found his man and at last Colonel Dwight

D. Eisenhower had his chance to prove himself in action. Later that month the following memorandum was sent through Third Army Headquarters at Fort Sam Houston:

July 19, 1941: "On and after this date, papers normally prepared for the signature of the chief of staff will be prepared: Dwight D. Eisenhower, Colonel, General Staff Corps, acting chief of staff."

Soon afterward it was followed by these orders:

August 7, 1941: "Colonel Dwight D. Eisenhower (O-3822), General Staff Corps, now on duty at headquarters, Third Army, San Antonio, Texas, is designated as chief of staff, Third Army."

Meanwhile, on August 5, Eisenhower, who had already arrived in Texas, wrote to Gerow:

"Next Monday I go to Louisiana and stay there until September 31 [*sic*]. All the old-timers here say that we are going into a God-awful spot, to live with mud, malaria, mosquitoes and misery. But I like to go to the field, so I'm not much concerned about it."

The Louisiana war games, in which Eisenhower proved just how great his talent for leadership actually was, were held during one of America's grimmest summers. The Axis armies, having thrust to the edge of the Channel, seemed capable of unlimited extension. From all sides there were warnings that the Japanese were preparing a blow in the Pacific. America's own military forces were hardly a match for the challenge they would inevitably have to meet and, on the eve of Pearl Harbor, the Louisiana games offered a poignant illustration of just what America's inadequacies were. But the Third Army, of which Eisenhower was chief of staff, acquitted itself brilliantly and despite its obvious shortcomings worked especially well with armor and air support. Its staff operated with exceptional efficiency. When the maneuvers were over, Robert Allen and Drew Pearson declared in their column, the *Washington Merry-Go-Round,* that "Colonel Eisenhower . . . conceived and directed the strategy that routed the Second Army." They added that he had a steel-trap mind and unusual physical vigor. By September 25, the Third Army was assured of overwhelming success, and that evening Eisenhower reviewed the situation in a long letter to Gerow:

General Krueger and I often talk about you. Particularly he spoke about the prospect of having you as one of the corps commanders in this Army. I suppose the Department will require you to command a division for a short time before you can be assigned a corps, but so far as I am concerned, I wish you were doing so right now.

There is a tremendous job facing every senior commander in this Army. The nervous energy and drive that are required in bringing a large unit along toward high training standards is tremendous; only people who are highly trained professionally and who have an inexhaustible supply of determination can get away with it. It is only rarely that the necessary qualifications are combined in one person. Some of them have plenty of drive but are totally unacquainted with training standards and methods in the smaller units, while others are technically proficient but have not the iron in their souls to perform the job.

One of the things that is causing the greatest trouble is that of eliminating unfit officers, of all grades and of all components. It is a hard thing to do, and in many cases it is too hard for some of the people in charge. But it is a job that has got to be done.

The last year has made a tremendous difference in the physical stamina of the men and in their ability to take care of themselves. Just before we started the problem in which we are now engaged, the tail end of a hurricane visited this section of the country and the Army got a good drenching. Yet when the problem started at noon yesterday, everybody was full of vim and ready to go. I do not know how long this problem will last but I can assure you that in armies of about a quarter of a million you can't do things in a hurry. You have to take time to unwind things, even for minor changes in plans and orders. . . .

I wonder if you heard a story that is going the rounds about some of the "simulated" things that are part of peace-time maneuvers. A corporal brought his squad up to a bridge and marched across it. An umpire yelled at him, "Hey, don't you see that that bridge is destroyed?" The corporal answered, "Of course I can see it's destroyed, can't you see I'm swimming?"

Stories such as the above float around and give us an occasional smile in spite of all the strain that goes with a job such as this. Handling an Army staff that has had very little chance to whip itself together has its tough points—in spite of which I am having a good time. But I would like a command of my own.

Instead of a command of his own, Eisenhower received a promotion. On September 29, the following message reached him:

THE PRESIDENT HAS SUBMITTED TO SENATE NOMINATION FOR YOUR APPOINTMENT AS TEMPORARY BRIGADIER GENERAL ARMY OF THE US STOP RADIO ACCEPTANCE IMMEDIATELY STATING ACCEPTANCE IS EFFECTIVE AS OF DATE OF APPOINTMENT STOP I EXTEND PERSONAL AND OFFICIAL CONGRATULATIONS

When Gerow wrote to congratulate him, Eisenhower answered with a characteristic paragraph:

Things are moving so rapidly these days that I get almost dizzy trying to keep up with the parade. One thing is certain—when they get clear down to my place on the list, they are passing out stars with considerable abandon. Nevertheless, I am glad to get it if for no other reason than I get some word from you as a result.

But beyond Gerow's congratulations and a few other similar notices, Eisenhower was still the same unknown officer whose picture had appeared in the papers a month or so before over the caption "Lt. Col. D. D. Ersenbeing." Except for his immediate troops and the handful of superior officers who were impressed by his excellent work, no one knew him.

The new general devoted November and the first week of December to cleaning up the details following the Louisiana maneuvers. Everything had to be in order by the middle of December for Eisenhower and his wife, Mamie, had arranged to visit their son, John, at West Point for Christmas. But by the first Sunday in December the war had begun; and on the fourteenth, Brigadier General Eisenhower arrived not at West Point but in Washington, where he had been called to accept a highly important staff assignment. This time he did not refuse it, for the orders came directly from General George Marshall himself.

From this point on, the course of Eisenhower's career moved steadily forward in the direction of Supreme Command. As he himself described it in *Crusade in Europe:*

I reported to General Marshall early on Sunday morning, December 14, and for the first time in my life talked to him for more than two minutes at a time. It was the fourth time I had ever seen him. Without preamble or waste of time the Chief of Staff outlined the general situation, naval and military, in the western Pacific.

The Navy informed him that the Pacific fleet would be unable for some months to participate in major operations. The Navy's carriers remained intact because they had not been at Pearl Harbor at the time of the attack, but supporting vessels for the carriers were so few in number that great restrictions would have to be placed upon their operation. Moreover, at that moment there was no assurance that the Japanese would not quickly launch a major amphibious assault upon Hawaii or possibly even upon the mainland, and the Navy felt that these carriers should be reserved for reconnaissance work and defense, except only when some great emergency demanded from them other employment. The Navy Department had given General Marshall no estimate of the date when they expected the fleet to be sufficiently repaired and strengthened to take offensive action in the Pacific area.

The garrison in Hawaii was so weak that there was general agreement between the War and Navy Departments that its air and ground strength should be reinforced as rapidly as possible and should take priority over other efforts in the Pacific.

At the time of the Japanese attack American army and air forces in the Philippines had reached an aggregate of 30,000, including the Philippine Scouts, formations integrated into the United States Army, but with all enlisted personnel and some of the officers native Filipinos.

United States outfits provided the garrison for Corregidor and its smaller supporting forts. Other American units were organized into the Philippine Division, which consisted of Philippine Scout units and the 31st Infantry Regiment. National Guard units—three field artillery regiments, one antiaircraft artillery regiment, one infantry regiment, two tank battalions, and service troops—had recently arrived as reinforcements.

The air strength had been increased during 1941, and on the day of attack there were 35 modern bombers, B-17s, stationed in the Philippines. Present also were 220 airplanes of the fighter type, not all of them in operating readiness. General Marshall knew that this air detachment had been hit and badly damaged during the initial Japanese attack, but he had no report upon the circumstances of that action.

There were known to be shortages in essential items of supply, but in the matter of food and normal types of ammunition it was thought there would be little difficulty, provided the garrison was given time to concentrate these at their points of greatest usefulness.

The Navy Yard at Cavite, just outside Manila, had been damaged very severely by Japanese bombers on December 10. That portion of the modest task force comprising the Asiatic Fleet which was disposed at or near Manila consisted mainly of small divisions of submarines. The largest warship in the Asiatic Fleet was the heavy cruiser, Houston, *at Iloilo.*

Against a strong and sustained attack, forces such as these could not hold out indefinitely. All the evidence indicated that the Japanese intended to overrun the Philippines as rapidly as possible, and the problem was to determine what could now be done.

General Marshall took perhaps twenty minutes to describe all this, and then abruptly asked, "What should be our general line of action?"

I thought a second and, hoping I was showing a poker face, answered, "Give me a few hours."

"All right," he said, and I was dismissed.

Significantly and characteristically, he did not even hint at one of the most important factors in the problem: the psychological effects of the Philippine battle upon people in the United States and throughout the Pacific. Clearly he felt that anyone stupid enough to overlook this consideration had no business wearing the star of a brigadier general.

I took my problem to a desk assigned me in the division of the War Department then known as "War Plans," headed by my old friend Brigadier General Leonard T. Gerow. Obviously, if I were to be of any service to General Marshall in the War Department, I would have to earn his confidence: the logic of this, my first answer, would have to be unimpeachable, and the answer would have to be prompt. A curious echo from the long ago came to my aid.

For three years, soon after the first World War, I served under one of the most accomplished soldiers of our time, Major General Fox Conner. One of the subjects on which he talked to me most was allied command, its difficulties and its problems. Another was George C. Marshall. Again and again General Conner said to me, "We cannot escape another great war. When we go into that war it will be in company with allies. Systems of single command will have to be worked out. We must not accept the 'co-ordination' concept under which Foch was compelled to work. We must insist on individual and single responsibility—leaders will have to learn how to overcome nationalistic considerations in the conduct of cam-

paigns. One man who can do it is Marshall—he is close to being a genius."

With that memory I determined that my answer should be short, emphatic, and based on reasoning in which I honestly believed. No oratory, plausible argument, or glittering generality would impress anyone entitled to be labeled genius by Fox Conner.

The question before me was almost unlimited in its implications, and my qualifications for approaching it were probably those of the average hard-working Army officer of my age. Naturally I had pursued the military courses of the Army's school system. Soon after completing the War College in 1928, I went to serve as a special assistant in the office of the Assistant Secretary of War, where my duties were quickly expanded to include confidential work for the Chief of Staff of the Army.

In these positions I had been forced to examine world-wide military matters and to study concretely such subjects as the mobilization and composition of armies, the role of air forces and navies in war, tendencies toward mechanization, and the acute dependence of all elements of military life upon the industrial capacity of the nation. This last was to me of especial importance because of my intense belief that large-scale motorization and mechanization and the development of air forces in unprecedented strength would characterize successful military forces of the future. On this subject I wrote a number of studies and reports. Holding these convictions, I knew that any sane preparation for war involved also sound plans for the prompt mobilization of industry. The years devoted to work of this kind opened up to me an almost new world. . . .

From tasks such as these I had gone, in 1935, to the Philippines. Now, six years later, I was back in the War Department, the nation was at war, and the Philippines were in deadly danger.

So I began my concentration on General Marshall's question.

Within a short time, he had an answer and returned to the Chief of Staff. "General," he said, "it will be a long time before major reinforcements can go to the Philippines, longer than the garrison can hold out with any driblet assistance, if the enemy commits major forces to their reduction. But we must do everything for them that is humanly possible. The people of China, of the Philippines, of the Dutch East Indies will be watching us. They may excuse failure but they will not excuse abandonment. Their trust and friendship are important to us. Our base must be Australia, and we must start at once to expand it and to secure our communications to it. In this last we dare not fail. We must take great risks and spend any amount of money required."

Marshall merely replied, "I agree with you."

Eisenhower continued to work on the Far East military problem throughout the early months of 1942, when the Japanese were moving almost at will in the Pacific and American defenses there as well as in Europe seemed hopelessly inadequate. Still he had his sights set on a troop command of his own, though now he aimed somewhat higher than the regimental level. On March 30, 1942 he wrote: "Par. 1–S.O. 79–W.D. announced me as major general. (Temporary) AUS–dating from March 28; ranking from March 23. This *should* assure that when I finally get back to troops I'll get a division–!!!"

Even on the very eve of his appointment to high command (he was to leave for London in June) Eisenhower had no inkling of what lay ahead of him. While it is clear from his correspondence and other writing that he had a full sense of his own capabilities, he hardly anticipated the use to which circumstances and the demands of history were to put them. By nature he was a confident man, with a keen appreciation of his own responsibilities and the limits of his capacity to fulfill them. But for the moment he knew that his duties were in the War Plans Division; he felt strongly that the present assignment demanded his full attention.

He spent many long hours at his desk and as a way of keeping track of the swift tide of enemy conquest, maintained a running commentary of events as they occurred. On his desk in the War Department was an appointment pad, die-cut so that a small clock was at its center and appointments could be written inside sectors ruled off by the hours. Eisenhower converted this pad into a makeshift diary, which he kept with some interruptions, day by day, until February 9. Some of these notes were of a general nature, suggesting an over-all plan for Allied victory. And others were more specific. But all of them illustrated two basic patterns in Eisenhower's character: one, his strict attention to the duties at hand, despite his own personal wishes and, two, his remarkable ability to organize a mass of complex information and set it down swiftly and simply for his own future reference.

On January 22, he wrote: "The struggle to secure the adoption by all concerned of a common concept of strategical objectives is wearing me down. Everybody is too much engaged with small things of his own—or with some vague idea of large political activity—to realize what we are doing, rather, *not* doing.

"We have got to go to Europe and fight—and we have got to quit wasting resources all over the world—and still worse—wasting time. If we're to keep Russia in, save the Middle East, India and Burma, we have got to begin slugging with air at West Europe; to be followed by land attack as soon as possible."

But more often the notes dealt with specific problems. On January 1 he had written a summary of the events to date: "I arrived in Washington December 14, 1941—telephone call from Office of Chief of Staff. I have been insisting Far East is critical—and no other sideshows should be undertaken until Air and Ground are in satisfactory state. Instead, we are taking on Magnet, Gymnast, etc. [Magnet was concerned with the movement of the United States air and ground forces to Northern Ireland as a backstop for the British and French forces in the United Kingdom, while

Gymnast was an operation planned against Northwest Africa on the Atlantic side involving only American troops, later enlarged to include the British and assault landings in the Mediterranean beyond the Straits of Gibraltar; it was the predecessor of Torch.] The Chief of Staff told me to pay special attention to Philippine Islands, Hawaii, Australia, Pacific Islands, China!" The following day he wrote only one sentence on the pad: "Unity of command in ABDA area seems assured. [ABDA stood for American-British-Dutch-Australian joint planning.] Good start! But what an effort. Talk–talk–talk!"

On January 3, there was another brief note: "Becoming increasingly apparent that something must be done in China. War efforts slowing down there and China shows signs of quitting. Apparently the British don't take this seriously. They should!"

The entry for January 4 indicated the frustrations and delays that hindered the Allied effort in the Pacific. "Tempers are short! There are lots of amateur strategists on the job—and prima donnas everywhere. I'd give anything to be back in the field. It's hard to get anything done in Australia. Dive bombers arrived minus essential parts [the Solenoids, 'trigger motors' for wing guns, had been fastened to the planes' crating and were thrown with the lumber on a scrap pile by inexperienced dock crews]—base facilities are meager. Other expeditions, directed by politicians, interfere, notably, Magnet and Gymnast. But we are getting some things on the way to Australia. The air plan is four pursuit, two heavy bomber, two medium bomber, one light bombardment groups. We are trying to ship staff and personnel needed. But we have got to have ships!! And we need them now."

And on January 5, there was a note of personal frustration, referring again to the business of a troop command: "Ham [Brigadier General Wade Haislip] is to go to a division soon as an assistant. Then later he gets a division to command. This War Department is cockeyed! Ham is one of our ablest—but he, at 52 or 53, must serve an apprenticeship *before* getting a division."

On Tuesday, January 6, Marshall was away for a day, but the pressure remained constant. "Chief of Staff out of town one day. Would be a relief except we have so much work can't catch up anyway. So we will go home at 10 P.M. as usual."

From then on the entries followed a more or less uniform pattern.

Wednesday, January 7: "Have been attempting to arrange better effect from China. Chief of Staff wanted to send ——— to organize air effort—Burma Road, etc. etc. Two days of feeling bum. Hope it's only flu. Afraid it may be shingles coming back!!" Thursday, January 8: "Still trying to get Navy to run the blockade (sub) into MacArthur, with some AA ammunition. Admiral King has issued orders—but I still am not sure we will get it done. May merely lose another sub." Friday, January 9: "Still working on China problem. Looks like ——— runs out of it. Wants none of it because he doesn't like the looks of things. He seemingly doesn't understand that we have *got* to do what we can with what we have."

Sunday, January 11: "Everybody has suddenly decided Far East is critical. Now we have all got to find some way to rush troops there—but *political* situation won't let us give up Magnet!!!" Monday, January 12: "Told Spaatz about trigger motors for A-24s in Australia on basis of MacA. radio. Said he hadn't heard of this before! Somervell [G-4] did a good job finding boats. We will get off 21,000 men on January 21 to Australia; but I don't know when we can get all their equipment and supplies to them. Ships! Ships! All we need is ships! Also ammunition—AA guns—tanks—airplanes—what a headache!"

Thursday, January 15: "Looks like Stilwell may be selected for China. That leaves Gymnast command open. Recommended three major generals and three brigadiers. Gee [Gerow] at top of B.G.s. I fear that the laborious nature of the procedure for sending a message to ABDA will drive us crazy! On *routine* and personnel matters we should have direct communication. G.H.Q. wants to start a campaign as far south as Freetown, Africa, working north. [An expeditionary force, working northward along the West Africa coast from Liberia, referred to in *Crusade in Europe,* page 43.] I disagree."

Saturday, January 17: "Colonel Hurley—former Secretary of War—is on his way to X [Australian base]. He was inducted at noon today—and at 1:00 tonight starts by plane via Pacific. He was equal to the quick transition and I am hopeful that he is successful in organizing blockade running for MacA. The whole Far East situation is critical. My own plan is to drop everything else—Magnet, Gymnast, Reserves in Ireland and make the British retire in Libya. Then, scrape up everything, everybody, and get it into N.E.I. and Burma. We mustn't lose N.E.I.-Singapore-Burma line so we ought to go full out saving them. We have been struggling to get a bunch of heavy bombers into N.E.I. but the whole movement seems *bogged down.* The Air Corps doesn't have enough men that will *do* things." Wednesday, January 21: "Catching a cold! Hope I can ward it off. Sent a long cable to Wavell asking advice on Dutch request for 600 pursuit planes."

Thursday, January 22: "Hurry-up call to go to State Department. Saw Secretary Hull, in conference with Navy files —Ridgway. Wanted . . . to give Chile . . . defense materials—so as to get a favorable vote for breaking relations with Axis. Scraped up a bunch of CAC—and small items of Lend-Lease ordnance. Arnold promised 50 A-6s or 17s for distribution in South American countries."

Saturday, January 24: "ABDA area boundaries changed some—for the better. Wavell now responsible for Darivi area. But what a job to work with Allies!! There is a lot of big talk and desk hammering around this place—but far too few *doers.* They announce results in advance—in a flashy way and make big *impressions* but the results often do not materialize and then the workers get the grief."

Sunday, January 25: "Spent the morning arguing with

Air Corps and G-4 showing them how B-26s can get to X a lot faster than planned. Sold them the idea and if we can get a little *drive* behind the thing maybe we can get some fighting strength in ABDA. For same reason have been plaguing Arnold about B-25s for Dutch. Saw Royce for a minute. Back from England."

Monday, January 26: "Australia, New Caledonia shipments supposedly leaving Charlestown today. Part leaves West Coast in couple days. Have never had much faith in New Caledonia garrison arriving there under current conditions. It goes *via* X. My own opinion is that the whole works will be so badly needed by ABDA we will never get this gang to Caledonia. However, we will see. In the meantime I am going to start making up another shipment for Far East. Got Navy and Air Force together on question of getting torpedoes to X for B-26s and making sure crews were trained in use. None of the people I talked to seemed to know anything about the matter; but now everything possible seems done."

Tuesday, January 27: "A Navy officer [McDowell] is trying to get us 'U.S. Secretary on Collaboration.' His duties are to clear the British on messages that require Combined Chiefs of Staff action. We sent to him, on 21st, an important message to Wavell asking advice on 26 pursuit ships. This morning we learn it has not yet even gone to *British here in Washington!* My God–how I hate to work by any method that forces me to depend on anyone else. . . ."

Friday, January 30: "The news from Wavell is all *bad!*

Troops in Malaya giving up and going back to Singapore Island *tonight.* The British still don't want Chinese. Wrote a memo today trying to smoke out the situation! What a mess. We are going to regret every damn boat we send to *Iceland* —etc. . . ."

Sunday, February 1: "Events move too fast and keep me too busy to permit the writing of notes! Day by day the case looks worse in ABDA. It is becoming clear that Jap damage to Sumatra forces is making it impossible for our B-17s to jump from Bangalore [India] to a satisfactory field in Java. Consequently our air strength is *not* building up as expected. The Navy made a raid in the Marshalls and Gilberts. Some damage was done to shipping and local defenses. One cruiser and one aircraft of ours sustained minor damage."

Wednesday, February 4: "We've decided to shift a group of pursuits from ABDA to Australia—for use in N.E.I. against Jap attack. Hope it does some good. Alerted the 2d Group to be ready for action to Australia. Hope it is in time. We made clear we wanted the arrangement to be temporary, so ABDA could get its planes back!" Thursday, February 5: "Had to change our priorities in sending planes to Australia! ABDA is desperate! Fields getting bombed! Lost 4 B-17s on *ground;* also 7 pursuits. We rarely lose a ship in the air, but my God how they do catch us on the ground. Burma situation not quite so gloomy, but Lord knows whether or not we can save the place. Gee [Gerow] and I have been yelling for the British to ask for Chinese help; but they (B) are certainly stiff-necked."

Friday, February 6: "Info that Chinese and British are finally getting together. We may save Burma yet! The Joint and Combined staff work is terrible. Takes an unconscionable amount of time. Fox Conner was right about allies. He could well have included the Navy! We are faced with a big reorganization of W.D. [Ordered by General Marshall before Pearl Harbor and carried out by General McNarney.] We need it! The G.S. is all to be cut down, except W.P.D.—which now has all Joint and Combined work (a terrible job), all plans and all operations so far as active theaters are concerned! We need help!" Saturday, February 7: "Mamie came yesterday. Living at Wardman. [Until then Eisenhower had been living with his brother Milton's family in Falls Church, commuting to Washington.]"

By the end of March, the critical points were disappearing, one by one, under the flood of Japanese conquests. On the last day of that month Eisenhower wrote in his office *aide-mémoire:* "For many weeks—it seems years—I've been searching everywhere to find any feasible way of giving real help to the P.I. We've literally squandered money; we wrestled with the Navy; we've tried to think of anything that might promise even a modicum of help. I'll go on trying, but daily the situation grows more desperate." The surrender of Corregidor, on May 6, ended the agony of the five-months-long defense. The United States had lost its last foothold in the Philippines and the spring of 1942 saw our military fortunes at their lowest ebb.

In February, Eisenhower had succeeded Gerow as head of the W.P.D. And as the latter was about to leave for a troop assignment, he said to Eisenhower, "Well, I got Pearl Harbor on the book, lost the P.I., Singapore, Sumatra and all the N.E.I. north of the barrier. Let's see what you can do."

Within a month Eisenhower added the entire ABDA areas to the list of Allied losses. Java was almost completely occupied, and MacArthur had already been evacuated to Australia. It now remained for Eisenhower to devise a plan for unified command in the Pacific. But while he applied himself to this task General Marshall was in England trying to establish the groundwork for Allied unity in Europe. When he returned in April he asked Eisenhower to make a careful survey of the situation and to return with a report outlining the set-up of a joint Allied operation in Europe. By June 8, the report, entitled "Directive for the Commanding General, European Theater of Operations," was ready, and when Eisenhower handed it over to Marshall he suggested that it be read in detail. Marshall replied, "I certainly do want to read it. You may be the man who executes it. If that's the case, when can you leave?"

Three days later Eisenhower had his orders. He was to leave for London and assume full command of the E.T.O.

Thus, in two short years Eisenhower, whose major ambition had once been to command a single regiment, had become commander in chief of what was to be in three years the greatest military force ever assembled. From among the entire roster of senior United States Army officers he was chosen to lead the Western powers in a desperate struggle for survival. What accounts for this phenomenal appointment?

As in all human events, accident certainly played a part. Had Eisenhower accepted Gerow's original offer and gone to Washington in 1940, he might never have been chosen by Krueger and Clark to serve as chief of staff of the Third Army. And had he never had this opportunity, perhaps he would not have been able to demonstrate his gift for leadership and organization at the very time the country was most desperately in need of it. Had he stayed at Fort Lewis, eventually to get the regiment he wanted, he might conceivably have remained a troop commander throughout the war.

But accident by itself was only a minor factor, for to a remarkable degree Eisenhower achieved his own destiny by his own devices. Very little of it was fortuitous. None of it was unearned.

First of all, he was a man of great professional competence, with a deep sense of world politics. He knew how wars should be fought and he knew that wars involved much more than strategy and tactics. As far back as September 3, 1939, when Chamberlain announced that Britain was at war with Germany, he had written:

This evening we have been listening to broadcasts of Chamberlain's speech stating that Great Britain was at war with Germany. After months and months of feverish effort to appease and placate the mad man that is governing Germany, the British and French seem to be driven into a corner out of which they can work their way only by fighting. It's a sad day for Europe and for the whole civilized world—though for a long time it has seemed ridiculous to refer to the world as civilized. If the war, which now seems to be upon us, is as long-drawn-out and disastrous, as bloody and as costly as was the so-called World War, then I believe that the remnants of nations emerging from it will be scarcely recognizable as the ones that entered it. Communism and anarchy are apt to spread rapidly, while crime and disorder, loss of personal liberties, and abject poverty will curse the areas that witness any amount of fighting. It doesn't seem possible that people that proudly refer to themselves as intelligent could let the situation come about. Hundreds of millions will suffer privations and starvation, millions will be killed and wounded because one man so wills it . . . power-drunk egocentric . . . one of the criminally insane . . . the absolute ruler of eighty-nine million people. And by his personal magnetism, which he must have, he has converted a large proportion of those millions to his insane schemes and to blind acceptance of his leadership. Unless he is successful in overcoming the whole world by brute force, the final result will be that Germany will have to be dismembered. . . .

But Eisenhower was more than simply a talented officer who comprehended the larger meaning of his profession.

He was a remarkably energetic person as well. He was capable of great good humor and he understood individuals as keenly as he did nations. Still more, he understood himself. He knew his powers and he knew his limitations. He knew his responsibilities and he knew his ambitions. During those long, wet months at Fort Lewis, when he was convinced that the world sat on the rim of a volcano and when he felt that he could serve both his country and his profession best by leading a regiment in the field, he stayed patiently at his desk, attending to his routine assignments, thinking ahead to the time when at last he would have his own troops, and preparing himself thoroughly for his future responsibilities. When those responsibilities finally descended on him, he was indeed prepared. But the preparation had been underway from his childhood. It began in Abilene and it continued through West Point and the service schools. He grew in leadership during his long and difficult years with MacArthur in the Philippines, and the complex process by which such growth increases continues to this day.

CHAPTER THREE

EISENHOWER WAS BORN close to the heart of America at a time when the country was on the threshold of its maturity. The United States in 1890 was in a frenzy of expansion, settling its wilderness, establishing the groundword for its industrial economy, expanding its population, and imparting its formidable influence to all corners of the world. Abilene, Kansas, where Eisenhower lived from the time he was a few months old, was a microcosm of this growth —a raw and confident city of nearly four thousand people. A bleak dusty place, still showing signs of the frontier, it was split down the middle by the tracks of the Union Pacific and Sante Fe. The north side of town was comparatively prosperous. The doctors, lawyers, and businessmen lived there. Eisenhower, whose parents were poor, lived on the south side, but attended school on the north. Apparently, however, his lack of social position made no difference in his early academic career, for he did well in school, especially in history, which he seems to have enjoyed considerably. He worked with harvest crews and in a creamery, and in his spare time he played baseball and football.

The fact that his family had little money and no position seems hardly to have concerned him, for it must be remembered that Abilene was a lusty youngster of a town whose inhabitants felt themselves capable of infinite possibilities. The rigid class structures that were eventually to calcify in such communities had not yet shown themselves and poverty was, as yet, no disgrace. Instead it was a challenge. Just as the spirit of the age had freed Eisenhower from the strictures of his family's sectarianism it taught him that he was capable of continuing growth as long as he applied himself to his work and heeded the dictates of his own conscience. As a typical young man of Abilene, he grew up with an abiding sense of his own direction and the unspoken conviction that he could, if only he applied himself, steer whatever course he chose.

Eisenhower never forgot the lessons that he learned in Abilene and he has frequently referred to them in later life. For example in June 1945, when he was called upon to deliver an address in London's Guildhall, the core of his message came in these words:

In the superficial aspects by which we ordinarily recognize family relationships, the town where I was born and the one where I was reared are far separated from this great city. Abilene, Kansas, and Denison, Texas, would together equal in size possibly one five-hundredth of a part of great London. . . . Yet kinship among nations is not determined in such measurements as proximity of size and age. Rather we should turn to those inner things—call them what you will—I mean those intangibles that are the real treasures free men possess. To preserve his freedom of worship, his equality before the law, his liberty to speak and act as he sees fit, subject only to provisions that he trespass not upon similar rights of others—a Londoner will fight. So will a citizen of Abilene. . . .

The exuberant determination, the informality, and the straightforwardness that Abilene impressed upon him mark his career from beginning to end. In his 201 file—which is a soldier's personal record of his career—he keeps as the first entry the graduation roster of his eighth-grade class in grammar school.

As Abilene knew him in his teens, Eisenhower seemed to be just another boy. If he was physically self-assured and a good student, there were dozens of others like him. But Swede Hazlett, one of his boyhood friends who is now a captain in the Navy, claims to have seen the quality of leadership in him from the start. In a long memorandum concerning his recollections of young Eisenhower he wrote:

Ike was somewhat more than a year older than I, and lived in a different part of town, so went to a different grammar school. Accordingly, although I knew him and liked him, I never knew him intimately until we landed in the same high school. Here he was not only an excellent student but, what was more important in my eyes, the star halfback of the football team—what would be known as the "triple-threat" nowadays. But I liked him most for his sterling qualities—he was calm, frank, laconic and sensible, and not in the least affected by being the school hero.

I early set my goal as West Point and had corresponded with my Congressman since I was twelve, seeking an appointment that never materialized. In the late spring of 1910 my Congressman offered me an appointment to Annapolis. I left school to prep at a cram school for the June exam. But the time was too short—I failed in mathematics. My Congressman kindly reappointed me. For I had seen just enough of Annapolis to be tremendously enthusiastic about it.

I went back to Abilene and got a job managing the office of a very small manufacturing concern. Ike had graduated from high school in 1909 and, because of lack of funds, had taken a job in the local Belle Springs Creamery. Eventually Ike expected to go to Kansas University (I have no idea what he intended to take up) but he felt it necessary to build up a nest egg first. He did very well in the creamery and in the summer of 1910 was made the night foreman, having entire charge from 6 P.M. to 6 A.M. True, he had only a couple of men under him, to keep the boilers and refrigerating plant running and to guard the plant, but it was considered a quite responsible job for a youngster only nineteen years old.

This summer I spent many of my evenings at the creamery,

helping him to while away the hours. We played a bit of penny-ante poker—giving him the start that ended in his reputation as the best stud player in the Army. Still being kids, more or less, we also weren't above raiding the company's refrigerating room occasionally, for ice cream, and for cold storage eggs and chickens which were cooked on a well-scrubbed shovel in the boiler room.

During this period our friendship grew very close. There was something fine about him that drew me to him—as it is drawing so many today. He had qualities of leadership of the best sort, combined with the most likable human traits—candor, honesty, horse-sense and a keen sense of humor. Naturally I talked a good deal about the Naval Academy, and gradually he became interested. At last it dawned on me that nothing could please me more than to have him go to the Academy with me. So I proposed to him that he try for an appointment, too. He was intrigued with the idea, but not very sanguine.

"What chance have I got?" he asked. "You already have the only vacancy from this district."

I suggested that he might try the Senators, and he was interested enough to write them both. One had no vacancies, but the other (I believe it was Senator Bristow) wrote that he had vacancies both for Annapolis and West Point. As was very unusual in those days when most appointments were political cumshaw, he was holding competitive exams for them, and he authorized Ike to appear in Topeka in November to compete. It was already September, so he had but little time to prepare. Here was where I came in—again. I had been studying for the same type of exams all summer, and was well up in the methods and short cuts of the cram school, so we started working together. Every afternoon at about two Ike would come to my office and we would work until about five. During these three-hour periods I managed to sandwich in enough office work to keep my job, but not much more. Ike's God-given brain sped him along and soon he was way ahead of his self-appointed teacher. In November he journeyed to Topeka and competed with about twenty other applicants. He returned, confident he had done his best, but none too confident of the outcome. That's another trait of his—he always puts forth his best efforts, but never underrates the opposition.

One afternoon he came into the office, grinning that wide, heart-warming grin of his, and waving a letter. The Senator wrote that he had stood first *in the exam. But there was a catch in it. He also wrote that, inasmuch as the West Point exams were in January while the Annapolis exams weren't until April, and as Ike was the best prepared of all his appointees, he was giving him the appointment to the Point. This was a cruel blow, and Ike didn't like it any better than I did. All his hopes had been aimed at Annapolis and he felt that, through me, he knew a good deal about it. I urged him to write the Senator and tell him that he greatly preferred the Navy, and beg for a reconsideration. He muttered something about "not looking any gift horse in the mouth," but he toyed with the idea for some time.*

Finally all question as to what he would do was settled by new information. The age limits for entrance to Annapolis were listed as sixteen to twenty, and we had mistakenly assumed that that included up to the twenty-first birthday. Suddenly, on rereading the pamphlet, I stumbled on the fact that one must enter before his twentieth birthday. I don't remember exactly when Ike's birthday comes, but think it is November. [Swede missed by a month; the date is October 14]. At any rate, he would have been twenty before entering in June. Birth certificates weren't required at that time and he could easily have knocked off a couple of years without anyone being the wiser—but of course he refused to consider any such stratagem. The age limits for West Point were eighteen to twenty-two—so that decided it beyond any further question.

We continued studying (and playing) together until January, when he took his entrance exams and passed with flying colors.

Thus from the very beginning Eisenhower's choice of an Army career was impelled partly by an accident. West Point, the first stage on the long road to Supreme Command, was not his original choice, but once circumstances had turned him in the direction of the Army, he applied himself with characteristic adaptability to military life.

But he was not an exemplary cadet. Just as the routine assignments at Fort Lewis were later to conflict with his desires to get out in the field with troops, so the rigid discipline of

West Point frustrated the robust, carefree attitudes he had acquired as a boy on the Kansas plains. One of his tactical officers at West Point, who remembers him best as a frequent violator of academy discipline, said of him once: "We saw in Eisenhower a not uncommon type, a man who would thoroughly enjoy his army life, giving both to duty and recreation their fair values [but] we did not see in him a man who would throw himself into his job so completely that nothing else would matter."

More than once the exuberant Eisenhower, finding it hard to accustom his Midwestern spirit to the harsh formalities of life at the Point, ran afoul of the honor code and was obliged to report himself for infractions of rule deliberately and willfully committed. His conduct record was far from good, but it indicated not so much an inherent perversity in the face of discipline as a strong streak of individualism.

One of the more amusing examples of Eisenhower's independence occurs in a story he likes to tell about his cadet days. It concerns a stuffy cadet who maintained a spotless conduct record at the Academy. It was a pleasure to rib him and one night Eisenhower went to his room, banged sharply on the door and asked to be admitted. When the cadet saw who his visitor was, he planted himself solidly across the doorway and urged him to go away. But rather than leave, Eisenhower took a package of Bull Durham from his pocket and began to roll a cigarette. The cadet was dismayed. Breathlessly he urged Eisenhower to take his tobacco farther down the hall. Instead Eisenhower stood pat, dragging deeply on his cigarette and filling the room with smoke. Finally, as Eisenhower descended the stairs, he turned and saw the cadet, his door flung open, vigorously dusting the corridor floor to remove any evidence of the ashes and tobacco scraps that had fallen there.

Many years later, when Eisenhower had assumed command of the North Atlantic Treaty Armies, the name of this same cadet, who had become a major general in the course of time, came up in conversation. "You know," Eisenhower said, "I still can't understand how —— got those two stars. He's always been afraid to break a regulation."

If Eisenhower was not a model cadet, at least he was a first-rate athlete and a good, if somewhat erratic, student. His athletic record was outstanding and until he injured his knee in a football game with Carlisle on November 9, 1912, he was one of the best quarterbacks West Point ever had. In academic matters, however, he was somewhat less distinguished, but still he held his own. He was weak in mechanical drawing and various other engineering subjects, but in English and history, which required imagination rather than mathematical exactitude, he stood near the top of his classes. On the other hand, there was a slight but extended deterioration throughout his four academic years. At the end of his plebe year he was fifty-seventh among 212 cadets; the next year he was eighty-first among 177; and at graduation he was sixty-first among 164 survivors of the original 212. Moreover, on the morning of June 12, 1915, when he received his commission, there were 124 of his classmates who could point to better conduct records than his own.

Eisenhower was obviously not one of the "great" cadets who from time to time have graduated from the Academy. When he received his commission there were few if any signs of the talent for leadership that was eventually to mark him as one of the foremost figures of his age.

Most of his classmates remembered him more as a good fellow and an outstanding athlete than as a brilliant officer. But he was an enthusiastic and personable young man, happy to be a soldier and eager to be a good one.

He was also handsome, and when his first orders sent him to San Antonio in the summer of 1915, he was in more or less steady demand at the various social functions in the city. At one of these he met his future wife, Mamie Doud, daughter of a prosperous Denver family that was summering in Texas. And within a year he married her.

Almost from the moment of his marriage he began conforming to a pattern he had never known before. Specifically, he lost the spirit of prankishness by which his independent nature had manifested itself throughout his term at the Point. He did not lose his independence by any means, but from July 1916 on, it was to take a different form, receding more and more deeply within him and becoming not so much a surface characteristic as a vital part of his inner nature. Mamie Eisenhower was a determined woman—as determined in her own way as her husband was—and her foremost desires were a home and family. She wanted a domestic arrangement which, despite the vagaries of Army life, would give herself and her husband a tangible basis for their marriage, and to this end Eisenhower bent himself with all the vigor he could muster.

But there were other considerations besides his marriage which contributed to this new sobriety. The country was clearly in danger. The isolation that it had enjoyed throughout the nineteenth century disappeared suddenly under the impact of the war in Europe and, as the pressure mounted, Wilson's last hope to maintain neutrality faded. By April 1917 we were in it and Eisenhower's responsibilities as a soldier at war grew heavier by the day.

From San Antonio, where he was stationed when Wilson's Congress declared war, he was sent to Leon Springs, Texas, and from there to Fort Oglethorpe, Georgia, to serve as an instructor in an officers' training camp. Apparently, he was very impressive in this capacity for throughout the next year he moved from post to post, training men to fight overseas. He left Oglethorpe on December 12, 1917, and was ordered to Fort Leavenworth, where he became an instructor in the Army Service Schools until February 28, 1918. Then he went to Camp Meade, Maryland, to help organize the 65th Battalion engineers. Finally, he was ordered to Camp Colt, Pennsylvania, where, with the rank of captain, he was literally to command the only Tank Corps training camp in the United States.

It was an exciting assignment for a young officer, but Eisenhower received it with mixed emotion. On the credit side was the fact that now, at last, his wife and his six-months-old son, who had been born in San Antonio, could join him. At the same time, however, the Camp Colt command made an overseas assignment for which he had been hoping seem more remote than ever. His immediate problem was the fact that at Camp Colt, which held 6,000 men ready and willing to submit themselves to the most rigorous training (for the tank was, after all, a novel and exciting weapon at the time), there was not a single tank to be had, with the exception of a solitary French Renault, until after the armistice.

Nevertheless, Eisenhower moved his family into a cottage in nearby Gettysburg and settled down to the somewhat puzzling challenge that lay before him. Under the circumstances he did remarkably well, drilling his men thoroughly, if not in the practices of tank warfare, at least in its theory. In the course of his service there he was promoted to major and then, on October 14, to lieutenant colonel. His progress upward was rapid but well deserved. Camp Colt acquired a first-rate reputation and its commander impressed not only his superior officers but the men who served under him.

Many of these men have never forgotten their young commander. As long ago as October 1943 the following notice appeared in a Washington paper under the heading EISENHOWER URGED FOR PRESIDENT:

New York, Oct. 4 (INS). *Tank Corps Post No. 715 of the American Legion in New York City went on record last night as determined to boost the candidacy of Gen. Dwight D. Eisenhower for President of the United States.*

A resolution to that effect was adopted by the post September 21, but not made public until now. The resolution said the members of the post had "no knowledge or concern as to the political affiliations or beliefs" of General Eisenhower but considered him presidential timber by reason of his outstanding "leadership qualities."

Many of the men who put forth this proposal were all World War I alumni of Camp Colt.

By the fall of 1918 Eisenhower had lost nearly every trace of his youthful recklessness. Along with almost everyone else in the country he buckled down under the pressures of his wartime responsibilities. The young lieutenant colonel disciplined his men firmly but not harshly. He drove them hard and himself still harder. But still he had time for his family and for the home that Mamie had made for him in near-by Gettysburg.

Nevertheless, when his orders to ship overseas arrived, he received them joyfully and prepared to leave Camp Colt for embarkation at Fort Dix on November 18, 1918.

Before he could leave, the Armistice intervened and Eisenhower remained in this country. He regretted having missed a chance to prove himself in battle, but his superior officers were quick to remark that he had acquitted himself brilliantly in his State-side activities.

Sometime after the war was over, the Adjutant General

wrote Colonel Ira Welborn, Director of the Tank Corps and Eisenhower's immediate superior, asking him to nominate any officers within his jurisdiction whom he thought worthy of the Distinguished Service Medal.

Welborn, a crusty officer of the old school who himself had won the Congressional Medal of Honor for exceptional heroism during the Spanish-American War, answered briskly and to the point.

1. In reply to your letter of January 23d and to circular letter of December 17, 1918, in reference to recommendations for the Distinguished Service Medal, you are advised that in the opinion of this office no officer under the direction of this office has rendered service so far beyond what should be expected of him as to warrant the award of a Distinguished Service Medal.

Then, thinking things over, he added:

2. However, since everything is relative, I would like to add that Colonel W. H. Clopton, Jr., Tank Corps, and Lieutenant Colonel D. D. Eisenhower, Tank Corps, have rendered especially efficient and satisfactory service under many trying difficulties as camp commanders and instructors of Tank Corps Units. If it develops later on that it is the policy of the War Department to award medals to officers for services in Training Camps, Depot Brigades, etc., I desire at that time to recommend the above named officers for Distinguished Service Medals, as I believe their services will com-

pare favorably with those of any officer on duty in a camp in the United States.

Lieutenant Colonel D. D. Eisenhower had no higher opinion of State-side duty than had Colonel Ira C. Welborn. He sent his father the official copy of the recommendation that had been forwarded to him for insertion in his 201 file, and wrote in pencil across the bottom of the sheet:

Dear Dad,

Just sending you above—as thought you'd be interested. There is no chance of my getting one of the medals—but it shows Colonel Welborn's opinion of me.

Devotedly,

Son

Nothing happened for several years; Eisenhower's own flat statement about his chances seemed to be right. Then, in April 1921, Colonel Welborn heard of several officers awarded the D.S.M. whose contributions to the Army were, in his opinion, not equal to Eisenhower's. He wrote the Adjutant General:

1. I desire again to bring to the attention of the proper authorities, with a view to securing for him adequate recognition, the services of Major D. D. Eisenhower, Inf. [after the war he had reverted to a permanent rank], *during the World War.*

Again, a year later, he resumed the subject and this time got action. Almost with a sense of relief, the Adjutant General wrote the persistent Colonel on October 11 of that year:

1. With reference to your letter of May 18, 1922, in which you request reconsideration of the recommendation for the award of the Distinguished Service Medal to Major Dwight D. Eisenhower, Infantry, you are advised that the Distinguished Service Medal was awarded Major Eisenhower on October 7, 1922.

Welborn was delighted. The following day he wrote Eisenhower:

Dear Ike:
Congratulations! And many!
Am sending this as a sort of advance notice, thinking that channels might be slow in reaching you. I sent the information over to Sheets and asked him to let Mrs. Ike know about it. She of course will be pleased beyond words.
It may seem like a posthumous award—it has been so long coming—but that will soon be outgrown.
Am rushed or would write more.
Best wishes and shake on this.
I. C. Welborn

But Eisenhower came out of World War I with considerably more than the admiration of his troops and a D.S.M. In the first place, besides his family and the responsibilities of fatherhood, he had acquired a sense of himself as a man. He had a profession and he felt the need to perfect himself in it. Though his academic record at West Point had suffered from the diversity of his interests, his future schooling—and he was to spend many of his next twenty years studying the techniques of warfare—was marked by steady application and consistent progress.

He was still the outspoken, independent Midwesterner he always had been, but the amorphous exuberance of his youth was now crystallized and took several very definite shapes. His youthful prankishness became mature good humor. He still knew that certain aspects of military life, as well as of life in general, should not be taken with the high seriousness that they seemed to demand. But now, with six years of responsibility behind him, he knew more exactly which parts of his experience to take lightly and which not.

At the same time he had acquired a feeling for his own capacities and their best uses. Recalling the lessons that his early optimism had taught him, he learned to be patient in the face of the inevitable disappointments of adult life. And his individualism which once had led his West Point tactical officer to look skeptically at his chances for success in the Army, developed into an admirable self-confidence—the kind that is born of achievement and not mere aspiration. The arduous months at Camp Colt had taught Eisenhower to respect himself, to trust his own opinions despite the contrary views of those around him, but at the same time he learned to respect the opinions of others if they seemed to emanate from sound judgment and a clear understanding of the issues involved. Occasionally, even to this day, he loses his patience in the presence of unclear and unexact thinking and in his earlier years he must have seemed, from time to time, an intolerant, rather over-scrupulous man. But he was fussy only in appearance and in the face of deliberate confusion.

Essentially, Eisenhower is a warm person with an enormous capacity for sympathetic understanding. Indeed his charm was an effective catalyst in Camp Colt and later it was to prove one of the key factors in his successful amalgamation of the Allied forces during World War II. Even now it serves to diminish the traditional hostility which for years has divided the European nations and kept them from forming the sort of political alliance on which their survival depends.

Along with this warmth Eisenhower occasionally gives the appearance of a rather exacting strictness—an ineradicable vestige of his early religious training. Throughout his World War I training assignments he upheld a rigid standard of personal achievement and demanded of himself as well as of others a whole-hearted application to duty. He still believes firmly in self-determination and individual enterprise, for he has never forgotten that in the place where he was born the only enterprises that succeeded were those whose proponents worked with the full strength of their own minds and bodies.

It was with these characteristics that Eisenhower—who had not yet reached thirty—came out of World War I. They remained more or less constant throughout the following years and in the interim between the wars they were to see him through one of the most arduous trials of his entire career. For it was during this period that he proved first to himself and then to his superiors that he had the stuff of a supreme commander.

CHAPTER FOUR

FOLLOWING THE GREAT WAR the American people settled down to what they somewhat vaguely described as normalcy. For a year or two the country tottered indecisively, trying to find a firm base on which to construct its new program of normal behavior, and then, thinking it had found it in the equally ambiguous word prosperity, set off blithely in pursuit of good times.

Meanwhile Europe was in the process of a major political upheaval proceeding from the social and economic chaos that came out of the war. The so-called "balance of power" which, during the last half of the nineteenth century, fostered mutual respect, if not friendship, among the European nations had collapsed and in its place there appeared a number of power vacuums.

The most significant of these—as it later turned out—was in Germany, where a violent economic crisis left that once pivotal nation weak and helpless. In the course of the 1920s two major political factions fought over its remains. One were the Communists, who hoped to achieve a socialist revolution in Germany just as they had done some years earlier in Russia. The other were the extreme nationalists who eventually emerged as the Nazi party.

Though few Americans paid much attention to these developments, the future pattern of Western civilization, as well as the course of the next twenty years, were to depend upon their outcome. Nevertheless, in the 1920s the United States was concerned largely with itself. It took pride in the part it had played during the World War and felt that it had given enough of its attention to the Continent, which was, after all, many miles away and, in any case, far too attractive as a playground to seem important in more serious respects. American businessmen settled down to making money, and those comparatively few Army officers who remained in the service prepared themselves for a long spell of relative inactivity.

America had no ax to grind and no place in particular to go. But despite its self-assurance, it could by no means avoid the obligations of history. Whether it liked it or not, its own destiny was very much involved with that of Europe, and the handful of Army officers who, even during the twenties, worked on the major problems of military doctrine were in preparation for the most devastating war in history.

CHAPTER FOUR

During the fall of 1919 Eisenhower met Brigadier General Fox Conner, who, perhaps more than any other officer then in service, sensed the tragedy that was soon to overtake the world. He was convinced that the war just ended did not preclude the possibility of future conflict but had instead prepared the way for a series of wars arising from the unstable situation in Europe. Eisenhower, who when he first met Conner was at the Infantry Tank School at Camp Meade, was immediately impressed and throughout the rest of his career never forgot the lessons that the older man taught him.

He spent the following year at Meade where he and his family established themselves according to the solid domestic pattern that Mamie insisted upon. Their quarters served as an informal gathering place for the other officers on the post and gradually acquired the appurtenances of a real home. Eisenhower himself had become thoroughly accustomed to this sort of living and thrived on it. He was delighted by his young son and had the usual ambitious plans for the boy's future. But just before Christmas 1920 the baby fell ill and a day after New Year's he died. His death was a swift, stunning blow to his young parents, and Mamie, whose youthful vitality seemed so much a function of her son's presence, never quite regained the effervescence that went out of her life during that Christmas holiday. There was little in their lives to soften the blow. And in their extremity they grew closer together, confirming the bond that had been established at the time of their marriage.

In July 1920, Eisenhower reverted to his permanent rank of captain and, in December of that year he was promoted to a permanent majority with rank from July 2, 1920. In January 1921, he graduated from the Tank School and assumed command of the 301st Tank Battalion.

Meanwhile, Fox Conner had been sent to the Canal Zone in charge of the 20th Infantry Brigade and asked if the young major and his wife would care to join him there. Eisenhower agreed and on January 7, 1922 left Camp Meade for Panama.

It was an instructive assignment for Eisenhower. Not only did he have a chance to study and help organize the Panama defenses at first hand, but he came under the direct tutelage of his brilliant superior, who, regarding his young assistant as something of a protégé, spent long hours with him discussing future military prospects.

He served under Conner for three years and by the end of that time came to regard him as a genius. The two men talked at length about the problems of unified command and the inevitability of another great war. And the core of Conner's logic came in the phrase, "We must insist on individual and single responsibility—leaders will have to learn how to overcome nationalistic considerations in the conduct of campaigns. . . ."

Thus another element added itself to Eisenhower's preparation for high command. Conner's discussions proved enormously provocative and Eisenhower read at length in the various source materials which the general recommended. He also looked forward to attending the Command and General Staff School at Leavenworth, which Conner insisted was an essential part of a top commander's training.

Happily he still found time for more gentle pursuits, and his home life, which had hardly been disrupted by the move to Panama, was as reassuring as ever. Toward the middle of his three-year tour with Conner, his old friend, Swede Hazlett, who was then a submarine skipper, put in at the Canal Zone and he and Eisenhower spent three weeks together. Many years later, Hazlett recalled the visit in the following memorandum.

In 1923, when I was in command of a submarine and partaking in fleet maneuvers in southern waters, a burned-out main motor laid my ship up for extended repairs at the Submarine Base, Coco Solo, Canal Zone. Ike, then in the grade of Major after having been a Lieutenant Colonel during the war, was stationed at Camp Gaillard—a jungle post about midway of the Canal. Here I spent several week ends with the Eisenhowers—and interesting ones they were. Ike got me astride a horse again and we rode the bosque trails; and in the evenings—some more poker. This latter was bad news, for Ike and his Army friends set a much higher standard for the five-card game than the Navy. But what interested me most was his work. He was, if I recall correctly, senior aide [*chief of staff, in fact*] *to General Fox Conner and had been largely responsible for drawing up war plans for the defense of the area; he explained them to me with the enthusiasm of a genius. He had also fitted up the second-story screened porch of his quarters as a rough study, and here, with drawing boards and texts, he put in his spare time re-fighting the campaigns of the old masters. This was particularly unusual at a torrid, isolated post, where most officers spent their off hours trying to keep cool and amused. Don't misunderstand —Ike was no studious recluse; he missed none of the fun (he never did) but still he found time to prepare himself for the future. He loved his profession, and he took it seriously. Perhaps he had a touch of clairvoyance.*

After my ship was repaired I took him for a dive in Panama Bay. He enjoyed it thoroughly. I never had a passenger who was more avid for information. Whenever I was otherwise engaged he wandered through the ship, chatting informally with the crew—and they responded readily. I really believe that by the time he left the ship he knew almost as much about submarines as I did. That night we had a big party at the Union Club, with Mrs. Eisenhower, her sister and some others—and I sailed the next morning.

At about this time Mamie left Panama for Denver, where she gave birth to a son, and within a year of her return she and her husband began looking forward to an assignment in the States. The years in Panama had begun to show themselves in Eisenhower's disposition as well as in his physical appearance. He had lost weight and occasionally his temper grew short.

Both he and his wife were relieved when orders finally

arrived to return home, and after a visit to Abilene and a few routine assignments he eagerly awaited an appointment to the Command and General Staff School in Fort Leavenworth. In August 1925, he was ordered there.

The school at Leavenworth is and always has been tough. Competition was intense and the order in which the students graduated frequently indicated the nature of their future assignments in the Army. Stories circulated about the officers who had broken under the strain and even committed suicide —some of them were true.

Never before in his career had Eisenhower applied himself as diligently as he did at Leavenworth. When he was not attending classes he spent his time studying in an attic room whose walls were covered with tactical maps. In June, when the term was over, he stood at the top of his class—just as another student, George Marshall, had done eighteen years earlier.

Immediately the atmosphere in Eisenhower's quarters lost its tenseness. Mamie was jubilant and a friend named George Patton was equally delighted. As soon as he heard the news he sent a letter of congratulations, saying that Leavenworth must be a good school if a "HE man can come out number one."

Eisenhower's success at Leavenworth was, of course, a significant step in his preparation for the job that history was eventually to offer him. At the Command and General Staff School, he learned the practical intricacies of high command, but even more important he perfected his ability to deal rapidly with a complex mass of diverse information and reveal its meaning in the simplest terms.

The basic ingredients of his capacity for organization grew out of his practical Abilene childhood, but the decisive formalization of his techniques developed most effectively at Leavenworth. The Army War College which he attended soon afterward was easy by comparison. And there too he graduated at the head of his class.

By the end of 1926, his name was placed, beside that of George Marshall, on the General Staff eligible list. And within a year he had a new and interesting assignment which was to prepare him still further for supreme command. At Leavenworth he learned all that books and charts could teach him about the French battlefields of World War I. His new assignment placed him in even more immediate touch with this terrain.

The Battle Monuments Commission, to which he was appointed in January 1927, had been set up to gather material for a guidebook to the American battlefields in France during World War I. By the end of 1926, it had accumulated a vast collection of photographs, maps, statistics, tourist information, and general descriptive material. Eisenhower was given six months to put this material into book form.

Once again he was confronted with a task that called upon his rapidly increasing powers to organize a body of complex information and develop from it a coherent arrangement of its major themes.

As Kenneth Davis, one of Eisenhower's biographers, describes it in *Soldier of Democracy*, the successful completion of the assignment depended upon the following method.

As always when his mind was confronted with a confusion of variable factors, he was moved (1) to analyze the confusion into its "components" so that the factors themselves could be clearly realized; (2) to assign to some one factor the status of a constant or common denominator by which the variability of all other factors could be measured; and (3) to recombine the factors in a whole which had a clear outline and a central or dominant principle. It was a technique which denied validity to whatever fluid elements might be present in a problem; whatever could not be given a rigid definition was simply excluded from consideration . . . the result . . . was a guidebook on historical principles which is one of the best reference works on World War I that has ever been prepared.

Davis goes on to discuss the value of the work:

Two facts made Dwight's work here of particular importance to his future. One was that by the time the job was done he probably had as much detailed knowledge of America's military role in the war—of the strategy, tactics, and logistics of A.E.F.—as any man alive, not excluding the General of the Armies. The second fact was that his work was accomplished under the appraising eyes of that general, for Pershing was chairman of the Battle Monuments Commission. Ever afterward the general was one of Eisenhower's most enthusiastic sponsors.

A year later, after having completed some further studies at the Army War College, Eisenhower accompanied by his wife and son Johnnie left for France to study the battle-sites at first hand. For more than a year he covered the entire terrain from Brest to the banks of the Rhine, walking over each of the battlefields and making notes on every item of military interest. He came to know the towns intimately. He examined their narrow, stone-walled streets, where a few determined men could withstand enemy battalions for days. He covered those areas throughout the French countryside where tanks could roar forward indefinitely and where, in other places, a half dozen demolition charges could halt an onrushing army in its tracks. He investigated the transportation system with its vast marshaling yards and studied the French army, split by political and religious factions within its ranks. When Eisenhower left France in 1929 he knew enough about its terrain, roads, and towns to lead a warring army from one end of it to the other. He was well prepared for June 6, 1944.

The guidebook was originally intended for the use of American tourists. At the time it was written—when Hitler and his fledgling nationalist party were still in quest of power in Germany—few Americans suspected that its author would eventually be in a position to put its contents to grimmer use. Yet even in 1929, world affairs were moving in the direction of catastrophe. America was on the edge of a violent economic depression and, even more significant, it was about to undergo a drastic revision of its political system.

By the time the Roosevelt administration came in, it was

evident that prosperity had not in fact been just around the corner, and that normalcy was only an illusion. America was, at last, obliged to tighten its own belt and face up to the grim realities of the new age.

Meanwhile, Communism had consolidated its hold on Russia and was busy laying plans for international revolution. Though it lost its foothold in Germany, its leaders in Moscow looked forward hopefully to a day when not only Germany but the entire world would come under the Soviet banner. And in anticipation of this event they were carefully observing the seeds of conflict that were steadily growing between the new Germany and the nations of the West.

Still, however, the largest part of the American population, as well as most Englishmen, turned their backs on the threat. Hitler, they felt, was vicious but hardly dangerous. And Communism, though its principles and practices were abhorrent to most Americans, was more a nuisance than a menace. Wasn't America, after all, the greatest nation on earth? Hadn't it just fought the war to end all wars? Then why worry? There were more urgent problems to face. Prosperity in America had fled. There was a depression to combat.

Eisenhower, remembering the advice of Fox Conner, was hardly as sanguine about international politics as the majority of his countrymen. He knew that a war was making up somewhere along the horizon and, furthermore, he was by nature not one to brush Communism off lightly. He was, above all, an individualist, profoundly independent and thoroughly opposed to absolutism in any form. Dictatorship, whether of a single man or in the name of the proletariat, offended him deeply and even back in the early thirties he knew that conditions in Europe would soon prove the wisdom of Fox Conner's prophecy.

When the twenties ended, Eisenhower had acquired many of the qualities required of a supreme commander. Leavenworth taught him the intricacies of military doctrine and the Battle Monuments Commission assignment gave him a chance to test some of this theoretical information against the background of the battlefields themselves. Because of his own appreciation of the international situation, he was in a position to look ahead to a time when history would call upon him to test his qualities of leadership. That time was not very far off. Within a dozen short years the German armies were to roll across the defenseless Continent. But also within ten short years Eisenhower would be ready to meet their challenge.

There was still to come, however, one more major phase in his preparation for high command.

CHAPTER FIVE

UPON COMPLETING the Battle Monuments assignment, Eisenhower was ordered, on November 8, 1929, to a desk in the office of the Assistant Secretary of War. To all outward appearances it was a routine assignment involving the fortunes of a shrunken army. But the job had several interesting side lights. In the first place, it was the Assistant Secretary's responsibility to oversee procurement for the air and ground forces, and in this connection Eisenhower spent many months working directly with industry, surveying sources of raw materials and analyzing the labor supply. Moreover, in the course of this assignment he helped establish the Army Industrial College, which he himself eventually attended.

He enjoyed his work and was happy to be in the capital.

Several of his close friends were there and it was a good place for a family man to settle down. "I think Mamie is glad to stay in Washington," he wrote at the time, "and of course it's all the same to Johnnie."

War seemed a long way off. Even those officers who, like Conner, were convinced that eventually a European crisis would once again involve the United States in armed hostilities, were content to sit quietly, anticipating many more peaceful years. The stock market was the important issue in 1930. And everyone wondered where prosperity had gone. No one, except the Army itself, was especially interested in America's military establishment.

Yet, Eisenhower went about his work with the usual enthusiasm. He was excited by his assignment and eager to learn as much as he could about American industry. Furthermore, he had at last become a real family man, living in civilian quarters, seeing his wife and son daily. Except for a few details he was, to all outward appearances, an average American businessman, with a schedule not appreciably unlike that of any other energetic executive. Occasionally his work took him away from home for a few weeks at a time to survey one or another aspect of American industry. On one of these trips he covered the Southwest, trying to ascertain how much the Army could depend upon guayule to provide substitute rubber in the event that Malaya was lost to an enemy.

During the trip he kept a diary, a genial, relaxed set of notes, which revealed as much about himself as about the guayule supply.

CHAPTER FIVE

Tuesday, April 8. Left Washington at 3:20 P.M. *on Liberty Limited for Chicago . . . Turned in early–quite chilly. Wednesday, April 9. Arrived Chicago 9:10* A.M. *Had breakfast on train. Took Parmalee bus to Dearborn Station. Walked up street and saw a movie, which was* terrible. *Party Girl!! Bah!! Had lunch and got aboard Santa Fe train "Navajo." Getting warmer all the time and I feel sure I am going to wish for summer clothes. . . . Thursday, April 10. Up at 7:00 to get breakfast at Hutchinson. Played baseball in that town twenty-one years ago. Lunch at Syracuse after going through Dodge City . . . Boy, how hot it is. . . . Boy, 'tis hot. Saturday, April 12. . . . We stay in San Francisco two hours and then hit the trail again for Salinas where we are due at 1:00* A.M. *Sunday, April 13. Arrived Salinas as per schedule. We have connecting rooms and one bath. . . . About 9:00* A.M. *Dr. Spence called us up from Pebble Beach, where he lives. Invited us to stay at a club as his guests–we declined. . . . At 3:00* P.M., *we examined several fields of guayule from one month to seven years in age. To "Inn Santa Lucia" for dinner . . . home by 10:00 and to bed.*

Monday, April 14. Had a very interesting day. Mr. Williams called for us at 8:00 A.M. *and we went at once to the guayule nurseries, a short distance from Salinas. The principal officials . . . are undoubtedly high grade–intelligent and honest. They are very frank–and discuss failures as well as successes. They took us to many fields of guayule . . . about 1500 acres are owned by the company–about 200 acres are on a share and share or contract basis–the remainder is* *leased. Rentals run from $7.00 to $15.00 per acre per year. Much of that planted in former years is still on a* commercial *experimental basis. Consequently some fields (because of unsuitable types of plants) do not have as good stands as do others. However, the men now seem certain that three varieties (out of hundreds experimented with) are commercially practicable. One of these is particularly suited to irrigation methods. We have been promised a detailed map of region—cost sheets—pictures, etc. . . . Wilkes and I traced the process from shrub to completed sheets, ready for shipment. We are convinced (now) that this is a real and growing industry. Land values may prevent any great expansion here. . . . Went to a movie tonight. Punk, as usual. Lord, but they are banal. . . . Wednesday, April 16. Went to plant and gathered up some loose ends of information. . . . Saw Monterey—Del Monte—artists colony at Carmel—the Monterey Cypress grove—wonderful beaches—country clubs—homes, etc. This section (had one a lot of money) would be ideal for a home. Hope to bring Mamie there sometime. Friday, April 18. Arrived El Paso after a hot dirty trip. Cleaned up and went to Juarez for a bottle of beer. Ate dinner there. Most expensive bust I've been on this trip. Spent over $5.00. Won't do that again. Went to bed early—and read until 2:00* A.M. *Saturday, April 19. Went to post. . . . Fort Bliss. . . . Morale seems to be high—but everyone is terribly anxious about the pay bill. Wish I could be more optimistic about it—but I believe the chances are so slim that it would be only raising a false hope to tell people that "in Washington it is believed a pay* *bill will pass soon." Certainly if we don't get one soon we are going to get only those men in the Army who are sons of wealthy families. . . . Monday, April 21. Left El Paso at 12:40* P.M. *Hot dusty day. In Washington, and at the hotel in El Paso we were told again and again that we needed no passport or other official papers to make a trip into Mexico. Two hours before train time we found that we needed a "tourists passport" and out we flew to get it. This we finally did. After the train crossed the river we waited interminably in Juarez for inspection of baggage—passports, etc. etc. . . . Tuesday, April 22. Arrived Torreon, 12:20. . . . Wednesday, April 23. Spent morning examining guayule rubber factory at Torreon. . . . Left Torreon at noon for Cedros Ranch. We went by train . . . and then cross country 65–70 kilometers in a Chevrolet. Oh boy, what roads!!!! Arrived ranch 9:00* P.M. *Supper and to bed. Thursday, April 24. The general manager of the Ranch is Mr. Selden Kirby-Smith, a son of General Kirby-Smith of Civil War. Quiet, unassuming and gentlemanly. He is about 5'5" and has spent the major portion of his life in the wilds of Mexico. His wife is in El Paso where his children are in school. They come down in summer time. This* A.M. *we went out with Mr. Yeandle and Kirby-Smith in an effort to get an idea of the general nature of ranch. Total—1,800,000 acres. Largely desert. Supports a growth of palms—cacti—desert shrubs—etc. The ranch buildings (some) which were built in 1732 were located here because of a fine spring. Los Cedros means "The Cedars"—which at one time surrounded the spring and pond. The*

Spaniards had a silver mine here. Their buildings, viaducts, etc. are now in ruins, but recognizable. There are great piles of slag, which contain 9% lead. . . . The guayule experiments near the ranch houses have been fairly successful. . . .

Friday, April 25. We continued looking over the place—examining fields, etc. There are now four guayule extraction plants in Mexico. These are at Torreon (the largest), Los Cedros—Catorce and Cedrol. Two others have been abandoned. The combined capacity of these four plants is about 40,000 tons of shrub per year (12,000,000 lbs. of rubber) . . . Sunday, April 27. Left Cedros at 8:30 A.M. *to come to Catorce in Chevrolet. Six hours on a twisty, dusty trail. Luckily the sky was overcast and therefore we were not uncomfortably warm. Here we struck the railway again. . . . Monday, April 28. Today for the first time we went through a plant actually making rubber commercially. . . . The factory process (primary) is as follows. . . .*

There is nothing remarkable about these unself-conscious notes, scribbled hastily at the end of a hard day's work. They reflect a typical American sensibility—a man of simple tastes, eager to do his job well and return home as quickly as possible. When he had nothing else to do, he attended a movie and, like so many Americans, was frequently disappointed. Occasionally he stayed awake late and read. He hated to spend five dollars for supper and again like so many of his contemporaries he looked forward hopefully, but with reservations, to making more money. He admired the beauty of such places as Monterey and Carmel, but he was not at all upset to realize that he could probably never afford to live in them. He did, however, hope to show them to his wife someday.

This pervasive simplicity contrasted sharply with the formal elegance of the stylish young general who served at the time as Chief of Staff and with whom Eisenhower was in almost daily contact. In the early 1930s Douglas MacArthur was one of the few tangible evidences that America still had an army at all. His father had been a brilliant general before him, and he himself, having made a phenomenal record at West Point, was a shining example of military bearing at its best. Style meant much to him and though the Army itself received little public attention, its dashing Chief of Staff was a public figure.

Yet despite his mannerisms, he made a considerable impression on Eisenhower. Whatever his critics—and there were many of them—might say about his elegant posing, they could hardly deny that he was a brilliant soldier with a fine and original military intelligence. Serving under MacArthur, Eisenhower had a rare opportunity to assimilate the man's theories and to observe him as he directed the Army from its General Staff offices. In many ways, of course, the two officers did not see eye to eye. The differences between their personalities made close co-operation difficult, but as divergent as their views frequently were, these two men entertained substantial admiration for each other's military acumen.

Thus it was not especially surprising that in the fall of

1935, when MacArthur became chief military adviser to the Philippines, he asked Eisenhower to join him as his assistant. Just before he proposed this assignment, MacArthur, having ended his tour as Chief of Staff and preparing to leave for Manila, dictated the following letter to Eisenhower:

You were retained by the Secretary of War, and later by myself, on critically important duties in the Department long past the duration of ordinary staff tours, solely because of your success in performing difficult tasks whose accomplishment required a comprehensive grasp of the military profession in all its principal phases, as well as analytical thought and forceful expression. Through all these years I have been impressed by the cheerful and efficient devotion of your best efforts to confining, difficult and often strenuous duties, in spite of the fact that your own personal desires involved a return to troop command and other physically active phases of Army life, for which your characteristics so well qualify you.

In this connection I should like to point out to you that your unusual experience in the Department will be of no less future value to you as a commander than as a staff officer, since all problems presented to you were necessarily solved from the viewpoint of the High Command . . . The numbers of personal requests for your services brought to me by heads of many of the Army's principal activities during the past few years furnish convincing proof of the reputation you have established as an outstanding soldier. I can say no more than that this reputation coincides exactly with my own judgment.

But despite this expression of confidence, MacArthur did not prove an easy man to work for. Nor was the job itself a simple one. Indeed it was fantastically complicated, dependent upon countless variables ranging all the way from climate to manpower.

Under the Tydings-McDuffie Act, the Philippines became a commonwealth in 1936 and were to become a completely independent government ten years later. In preparation for this, the Islands' government had made provision for an army. Anticipating many of the problems that he would undoubtedly have to face in organizing this force, MacArthur ordered his staff to prepare a comprehensive Philippines Defense Plan well in advance of his scheduled departure for the Islands.

The original plan was drawn up by Major James Ord, an instructor in the Army War College. He was assisted by the faculty there and supervised by MacArthur himself in collaboration with his assistant, Major Eisenhower. The plan was based primarily on the maximum military establishment compatible with the Philippines' population, geography, and climate. Cost was secondary.

When MacArthur first saw the completed plan, he rejected it on the ground that it was far too expensive for Manila's infant government. Immediately Eisenhower and Ord went back to work and together they reshaped the plan, reducing training periods, cutting pay and armaments, discarding costly weapons, and substituting conscripts for professional soldiers wherever they could. They arrived at a minimum yearly cost of twenty-two million pesos, or eleven million dollars. MacArthur still thought the estimate too high and decided that the figure must be cut to sixteen million pesos, or eight million dollars.

Again Ord and Eisenhower went at it. They reduced the proposed professional force from 1500 officers and 19,000 enlisted men to 930 officers and 7,000 enlisted men. They extended the munitions procurement program through a twenty-year period instead of a ten-year period. They postponed an artillery corps indefinitely. And, finally, they arrived at MacArthur's desired estimate.

But despite the best efforts of its American officers, the Philippine Defense Plan was doomed from the start. Its budget—appallingly low even in 1936, when armaments were relatively cheap—was crippling. MacArthur wanted an army of 30 divisions, supported by 250 planes and 60 torpedo boats. Repeatedly his staff told him that he could never achieve his goal on the sums allotted him. Yet he persisted, apparently in the hope that he could eventually get the necessary funds from the Philippine Government when the need arose. But he was wrong. For four trying years, President Quezon held him to an $8,000,000 annual budget.

Meanwhile, the Philippines' political atmosphere, murky with cliques and factions, made progress difficult. An imposing façade of titles, uniforms, mobilization plans, paper divisions, and promises seemed to constitute great military achievement in the eyes of many Filipinos.

Eisenhower and Ord had not been unsuccessful because of lack of effort on their part. Tirelessly, they had maintained that success hinged on four factors: the construction of adequate facilities for the new army; the procurement of arms and ammunition; the training of a satisfactory officer corps; and the development of administrative machinery for the registration, induction, and discipline of the recruits. That much accomplished—and it would take several years to do the job well—the foundation and framework for the defensive force would be sound. However, even those preliminaries, which in retrospect sound like plain horse sense, could not easily be carried out. The first two—construction and procurement—had been crippled by their own budget-trimming back in Washington.

Complicating the construction situation still further had been the discovery, when the military mission reached Manila, that the reservations already allotted the defense forces were completely inadequate. Camp Murphy, near Manila, intended as an air base and flying school, a garrison for a regiment of troops, and a division headquarters, comprised little more than a hundred acres of land. Most of the other camps were so located as to arouse suspicions that the most valueless and inaccessible swamps in the Philippines had been fobbled off on the government.

In armament, however, Ord and Eisenhower hoped to ease

some of the financial stringency by procuring four hundred thousand Enfield rifles from the United States Government at a nominal cost. Because the rifle was practically obsolete for American purposes, they hoped to buy them for two dollars each, or less. But they did not make allowance for buck-passing in the War Department. Their proposal finally ended on the desk of President Roosevelt himself—in an election year. For weeks the matter hung fire while the War Department, High Commissioner McNutt, the Department commander, and the President of the United States played shuttlecock with the proposal.

After two months, Ord and Eisenhower feared that the question would be settled in Washington on a political basis with an eye toward the pacifist vote. Finally Washington compromised and agreed to ship a hundred thousand Enfield rifles during 1936, with the further understanding that if all went well an additional three hundred thousand rifles could be made available to the Philippine Government over a period of eight years. But, instead of two dollars apiece, the price would be nine dollars. Even so, the saving was considerable. Under ordinary circumstances Springfields would have cost approximately thirty-one dollars each, delivered in Manila. For a thirty-division army that would have meant twelve and a half million dollars or about one-sixth of the ten-year budget, leaving no money at all for bullets. In any case, the mechanical difference between the Enfield and the Springfield was small. The Enfields, delivered that fall, were used on Bataan a little more than five years later—the most effective survivals of the original Philippine Defense Plan.

A far more serious problem facing the planners was the establishment of an officers corps. Senior officers in the Philippines constabulary had considerable individual ability, but were without experience in the administration of large military organizations. The same was true of the Philippine Scouts, who felt that they were an integral part of the United States Army and looked with suspicion on the argument that they change uniforms. Thousands of officers had to be trained if the army was to have any leadership at all. Thirty divisions would require a general staff, special staffs, and a large service-school system—as well as an air force and its technical staffs, and a mosquito-boat navy. Two or three years at least were needed to build an officer corps. In the meantime, the complicated machinery for registration, induction, and administration of the conscripts had to be designed and tested on an experimental scale. By the end of 1938, everything was to be ready. In another three years, there were to be enough battalions of trained riflemen on every major island in the archipelago to hamstring a Japanese invasion. That at least was the plan.

Although short of money, arms, transport, and housing, the Philippine Army, at birth, suffered from too much man power. The speeches delivered by Quezon and others, heralding the Filipinos' readiness to fight their own battles; the glamor of America's most romantic military figure returning to the people whom his father had freed and whom he loved; and natural patriotism—all these combined to inspire nearly everyone who could pass himself off as twenty years old at his last birthday. At the first registration, in April 1936, 150,000 recruits were enrolled—a figure far beyond any reasonable forecast. The turnout was enough to arouse visions of serried ranks of Filipino soldiers in any number of divisions, ready to defend the home islands with their lives. Such spirit could not be rebuffed.

Without an officers corps, without buildings or training facilities, above all without work-horse corporals and sergeants, the Philippine Army choked in its infancy. Ord and Eisenhower spent their days in an endless process of whittling, substituting, and improvising, trying desperately to postpone the inevitable collapse.

By Christmas 1936, both men were fagged out. Most of the camps would not be ready for recruits in January. Still worse, many of them were on poor sites and had poorer facilities; several were without water, roads, or light. Worst of all, the great rush to get ready for the recruits boosted costs, which, even if they had not gone up, would have been much higher than originally estimated.

In the spring of 1937, MacArthur and Quezon were in the United States, where the President of the Commonwealth urged that Philippine independence be advanced from 1946 to 1938 or 1939.

While MacArthur and Quezon were away, the first draft of conscripts entered the army. Before their five and one half months' tour was over, all available funds were practically exhausted. With disaster immediately ahead, the American advisers—after MacArthur's return—spent their time in more revision of the budget.

The following year—1938—the Philippine National Assembly increased the arms budget by more than two million dollars and added nearly another two million for construction. However, even this temporary increase was inadequate. The estimated expenses were certainly going to exceed the budget, and, what was worse, the assembly was bound to be displeased by the apparent lack of results.

Moreover on Sunday, January 30, 1938, Jimmy Ord was killed in an airplane accident. Eisenhower at the time was in Sternberg Hospital, where Ord had visited him an hour before the crash. By his death, Eisenhower lost one of his closest companions, an invaluable working partner and one of the few really helpful members of the group.

Captain Bonner Fellers (later a general officer on MacArthur's wartime staff) was brought in to work on the budget. Once again, the emphasis was on an army overwhelmingly strong in man power—the new target was ninety divisions within thirty years. But the budget remained eight million dollars a year. Despite the Assembly's recent generosity, it would balk at any attempt to provide a permanent increase.

From July 26 to November 5, 1938, Eisenhower was in the United States with Mamie and John. In part, the trip constituted a leave; for two and a half years he had been overworking himself in the tropical heat and damp of Manila. He needed a rest. In part, the trip was a scavenging foray for surplus American equipment that could be begged for the Filipinos and a shopping expedition for bargains in mortars and artillery that the Filipinos would have to buy.

By 1939, the Defense Plan had collapsed completely. Eisenhower and the late James Ord had little to show for their sacrifices. During the spring of 1939, Eisenhower spent most of his time touring the camps in an attempt to combat the defeatism that was steadily draining away the last few drops of life left in the moribund army. On March 24, 1939, he said to the R.O.T.C. graduates of the University of the Philippines:

"So long as there exists among a nation's citizens a common and flaming determination to protect themselves and their homes against any invasion by force, they can, in unified effort, develop a formidable defensive power. The Philippine Defense Plan assumes that this spirit does exist and will continue to grow and flourish in these Islands.

"As a consequence of these considerations and assumption, the defense plan simply provides the machinery whereby the free citizens of this country may co-operate toward their own protection. They must be reasonably trained, properly equipped, well organized and efficiently led, so that they may be instantaneously ready in every province and barrio to line your beaches with the defensive fires that will beat back any attempted invasion."

For Eisenhower, the end came before the year was out. On December 12, 1939, President Manuel L. Quezon gave him an official luncheon at Malacanan Palace and awarded him the Distinguished Service Star of the Philippines. The citation read:

As the Senior Assistant of the Military Adviser from the inauguration of the Commonwealth to the present time, Colonel Eisenhower has continuously devoted his exceptional talents to the development of adequate security forces for the Philippines. Through his professional attainments, his breadth of understanding, his zeal and his magnetic leadership he has been responsible for notable progress in the Philippine Army. Through his outstanding achievements, in the service of the Philippine Government, he has increased the brilliance of his already enviable military reputation, and has earned the gratitude and esteem of the Filipino people.

On the following day, Eisenhower, his wife, and son sailed from Manila aboard the *President Coolidge* while on the dock waving good-by were the MacArthurs and scores of other American and Filipino friends as the Filipino Army Band played farewell. The Eisenhowers were returning at last to the United States Army, ready to face the great challenge that lay immediately ahead.

The Philippines adventure had been a mess from beginning to end—a hopeless tangle of political intrigue, personal vanity, and limited funds. But amid all the hopelessness, there was one positive note. The Philippines completed the final phase of Eisenhower's preparation for high command. In Manila's steaming confusion, the young American officer who only four years before had held a routine assignment in the War Department learned the value of diplomacy and the intricacies of statecraft. He had learned the problems of building an army from nothing in the face of political interference. And most of all, he knew at first hand the ins and outs of high command.

When he landed at San Francisco and from there proceeded to Fort Lewis, he had completed the major stages in his preparation for leadership. Now it was up to history to put him to the test.

CHAPTER SIX

THE GREAT CHALLENGE lay immediately ahead. As Eisenhower worked restlessly through the months on the West Coast he knew that the world was about to feel the full force of Fox Conner's prophecy. Once again the Continent had gone to war, and soon America would follow.

Eisenhower had come far since West Point. Through the years he had grown steadily in leadership, and the basic pattern of his Midwestern character was now colored by many years of long, hard experience. In the course of time he had perfected his military skills and sharpened the edge of his personality so that despite its continuing warmth and good humor it could cut through the entanglements of inefficiency and political intrigue. He retained the spirit of independence that he had acquired as a boy, but now it was tempered by years of working with expedients which frequently required tactfulness and compromise rather than direct assertion.

When, in the summer of 1942, he left the United States to assume command of the European Theater of Operations, he carried with him an abundance of the qualities of leadership. But he displayed few of the characteristics that conventionally mark the professional soldier. He had no ambitions for personal glory and he sought no new territories for his country. He came to Europe with the promise of peace and dedicated himself to concluding the war as swiftly as possible. He was sent by his country to assure the continued existence of a society in which free people could live and raise their families with dignity and security in the conviction that no harm would come to them as long as they worked honestly and respected the rights of their neighbors.

Unlike the Nazis or the Communists who promised the people of Europe bigger houses and better farms, Eisenhower assured them simply that when victory came they would have the right to retain the houses and farms they had always had and that, given a little luck and reasonable courage, they could hope to improve their situations by their own devices under the auspices of a democratic government.

Eisenhower brought more than an American army to Europe—he brought an American faith. The millions who fought alongside him knew somehow that they shared with him a common goal—that both they and their leader sought simply to preserve the security of each man's home and family. Never throughout the entire war did Eisenhower lose sight of this goal.

Even through the most trying campaigns, when disaster lay behind every hill and the problems of high command seemed hopeless, his mind turned to thoughts of home—his wife and son and the grandchildren he hoped to raise in a peaceful world. He seldom expressed himself openly on these matters—they were never the subjects of his public speeches. But often in the privacy of his own quarters he wrote a note to himself or to a friend that revealed his private feelings.

In November 1942, for example, he took a few moments from his packed schedule to write the following:

INCONSEQUENTIAL THOUGHTS OF A COMMANDER DURING ONE OF THE INTERMINABLE "WAITING PERIODS"

War brings about strange, sometimes ridiculous situations. In my service I've often thought or dreamed of commands, peace commands, battle commands, administrative commands, etc. One I now have could never, under any conditions, have entered my mind even fleetingly. I have operational command of Gibraltar!! *The symbol of the solidity of the British Empire—the hallmark of safety and security at home—the jealously guarded rock that has played a tremendous part in the trade development of the English race! An American is in charge and I am he. Hundreds of feet within the bowels of the Rock itself I have my C.P. I simply* must *have a grandchild or I'll never have the fun of telling this when I'm fishing, gray-bearded, on the banks of a quiet bayou in the deep south.*

In the absence of any grandchildren of his own, he occasionally took the liberty of writing to his brother Milton's young daughter. One day, after receiving a scribbled note from her, he answered:

Dear Ruthie:

I enjoyed your letter. I know exactly what you said. I am astonished that you have made such progress since I last saw you. Since I cannot write as well as you do, I will have to have this done on the typewriter, so your Mother may have to read it to you.

I know that by the time I come home that beautiful blue velvet dress that you got a year ago for Christmas will be far too small; but please keep it because I think that is the best-looking dress I ever saw in my life and I want to see it again.

With lots of love.

And in July 1942, he confessed to Milton himself just how much he missed his family: "It is a rather lonely life I lead; every move I make is under someone's observation. And as a result, a sense of strain develops that is entirely aside from the job itself. At home a man has a family to go to." For Eisenhower, home was wherever Mamie happened to be.

(Less than a month after V-E Day, he wrote in the same vein: "The last six weeks have been my hardest of the war. I presume that aside from disappointment in being unable to solve in clean-cut fashion some of the nagging problems that seem always to be with us, part of my trouble is that I just plain miss my family." He added that he had a chance to see his son, John, who was then with the First Division, about once a month, but he went on to say: "It is not the same thing as being able to re-establish, after three years, something of a home." He hoped that his wife might be able to join him eventually without causing his critics to accuse him of seeking special privileges. He hoped "that most people would understand that after three years continued separation at my age, and with no opportunity to engage, except on extraordinary occasions, in normal social activities, they would be sympathetic about the matter.")

But in the meantime there was a war to be fought, and if Eisenhower expected to return to his home and family, it would have to be fought well. The pursuit of victory came first. Germany had to be defeated and nothing could interfere with that goal. The future of civilized society depended on it, but there were enormous sacrifices ahead. Everyone had to contribute. Eisenhower outlined the situation as he saw it, in a letter to a friend who had complained bitterly that an ailment restricted him to State-side duty. On April 3, 1943, he wrote him:

Nothing that I can say can possibly ease your disappointment in being excluded from the more active phases of this war effort. However, as the responsibilities thrust upon me have become wider and heavier, I have come to appreciate more and more clearly how true it is that nations, not armies and navies, make war. Everybody has a job. Yours happens to be in a niche that does not completely satisfy all the training you have received, the experience you have gained, and the thought you have expended in the naval profession. But I am almost fanatic in my belief that only as we pull together, each of us in the job given him, are we going to defend and sustain the priceless things for which we are fighting. It seems to me that in no other war in history has the issue been so distinctly drawn between the forces of arbitrary oppression on the one side and, on the other, those concepts of individual liberty, freedom and dignity, under which we have been raised in our great Democracy.

I do not mean to sound like a demagogue or a politician. In fact, once this war is won, I hope never again to hear the word "politics." But I do have the feeling of a crusader in this war, and every time I write a letter or open my mouth, I preach the doctrine that I have so inadequately expressed above.

In the beginning, the Allied forces were beset with hordes of problems, many of which stemmed directly from inadequate training. Eisenhower worked tirelessly to bring his armies into fighting shape. But in the early stages at least he was far from satisfied with the results.

In the middle of January 1943, he wrote to Major General Russell P. Hartle, who headed troop training back in the United Kingdom: "Nothing has impressed me more in connection with our operations in this theater than our deficiencies in training . . . I have no great fault to find with our training doctrines or methods. Generally, they are sound. It is in the application of them that we fail. If only we can now, now that we are at grips with the enemy, impress upon our junior officers . . . the deadly seriousness of the job, the absolute necessity for thoroughness in every detail—then we will begin to get results. Seemingly we have been unable to do this. We must try again, and harder."

He pointed out deficiencies in discipline, in anti-aircraft defense, in conservation of rations, in marksmanship, in aircraft recognition, and in joint exercises of air and ground forces. "The mistakes made in maneuvers," he went on, "nearly two years ago are now being repeated on the battlefield—almost without variation—but this time at the cost of human life instead of umpire penalties."

Five weeks later, he was in the field near Kasserine. The same deficiencies were glaringly evident. He ordered immediate changes. They came too late. Before they could be put into effect, Rommel struck. For days, the Tunisian campaign was in jeopardy. At his advance command post, the commander in chief watched over the battle until the thrust was turned back.

On his desk, when he returned to headquarters, was a letter from his friend General Gerow. Eisenhower answered:

I got back this morning from the battlefront. I wish that every division commander in the United States Army could go up there right now and see the consequences, the appalling consequences of failure to achieve in advance some measure of battlefield discipline, to teach his men the essentials of scouting, patrolling and security, to insist upon initiative on the part of every leader from corporal up . . . I feel so strongly on this subject that I could write reams . . . The only thing on which I would venture to give advice is that you must be tough. You may not be able to discover among your men those that will be the best battle leaders, but you can find those who are this minute endangering the battle success of your whole command. They are the lazy, the slothful, the indifferent, the complacent. Get rid of them if you have to write letters the rest of your life . . . For God's sake, don't keep anybody around of whom you say to yourself, "He may get by"—he won't. Throw him out . . .

He was a firm commander and occasionally, when confronted with the results of carelessness, a furious one. But he never lost his sense of proportion. He knew the physical limits of the men under him and understood intimately the enormous pressures that they faced every day. Once after dictating an angry memorandum concerning the laxity of some of his troops and berating their tendency to enter squabbles with their fellow soldiers rather than concentrate on the enemy, he concluded with the following paragraph.

I realize that everybody has been working at top speed and under conditions of great strain. Many points that would normally be taken care of automatically or would never even arise have become a bit noticeable here because of a variety of conditions that are practically beyond any human control. All I demand is that every man do his best; and if he does that, he need have no fear of his standing with his superiors and [*no lack*] *of the certainty that he will be constantly brought up to serve in positions of increasing responsibility and authority. We must all realize that we are fighting a tough war and everything we do, day and night, must be directed toward the winning of that war. Training, morale, self-respect, smartness, saluting, respect for Allies—each of these subjects has, in its own way, some bearing upon the efficiency of an army. That is what I am interested in.*

Frequently, he himself felt the strain of endless days and nights of unrelenting concentration. The rigid discipline he imposed on his men, he imposed on himself as well. Two days before the Tunisian Campaign ended, he wrote General Marshall:

Sometimes I think it would be most comforting to have a disposition that would permit relaxation—even possibly a feeling of self-satisfaction—as definite steps of a difficult job are completed. Unfortunately, I always anticipate and discount, in my own mind, accomplishment of the several steps and am, therefore, mentally racing ahead into the next one. The consequence is that all the shouting about the Tunisian Campaign leaves me utterly cold. I am so impatient and irritated because of the slowness with which the next phase can unfold that I make myself quite unhappy. I am convinced that if I could undertake Husky [the invasion of Sicily] *today with only two divisions, I could gain a bridgehead and an advantage that would make the further conquest a very simple affair. Just as I suffered, almost physically, all during January, February and March while the enemy was fortifying his positions in Tunisia, so now I resent every day we have got to give him to perfect and strengthen Husky defenses. I have gotten so that my chief ambition in this war is finally to get to a place where the next operation does not have to be amphibious, with all the inflexibility and delay that are characteristic of such operations.*

Four days earlier, a courier had brought him a letter from General Marshall, in which the Chief of Staff passed on a word of advice:

At the moment there has come to my hand a letter of urgent advice for you written by Mr. John A. Petroskey of Lyon Mountain, New York, Box 157. In brief he says this, which I pass on to strengthen you in your current battles: he has "just learned that one of our most important men, General Eisenhower, takes cold water with his meals." He states that "Many nations and Armies have gone down in defeat on just such an insignificant point and we cannot afford to let a brilliant mind like General Eisenhower's be hampered by his stomach!" He asks me to forward his letter to you as soon as possible, and to advise you that "General Rommel would not have been the successful desert fox if he was caught with a cylinder or two missing in his brain by bad indigestion."

After you have cut out the cold water I expect to see modified Husky go through with a bang and the Germans left in the desperate plight of the Cape Bon peninsula.

Concerning the recommendation, Eisenhower replied:

. . . I am still, I think, a bit of a puzzle to my British confreres because I refuse wine, but this is the first time that any comment has been made about my drinking water. Actually my health was never better. For the past three weeks, I have been getting in some five or six hours a week of rather vigorous riding, which represents the only exercise I have had since the war started. The only difficulty I have at all is sleeping in the later hours of the night. I have developed a pernicious habit of waking up about 4:00 to 4:30, and finding that I am sufficiently rested to begin wrestling with my problems. Once in a while I have been able to put myself back to sleep.

But he had more to reckon with than his own capacity for work and that of his men. His responsibilities grew greater by the day, and on Christmas Eve 1943 President Roosevelt announced that Eisenhower had been chosen to command Overlord. His new title was Supreme Commander, Allied Expeditionary Forces, and his immediate task was to prepare for the forthcoming invasion of Normandy.

There were larger problems involved in this assignment than simply the organization of an Allied landing force. Most disturbing, perhaps, was Winston Churchill's conviction, continuing even after the Overlord decision, that Germany must be assaulted through the Mediterranean "soft underbelly," preferably by way of the Balkans. According to Eisenhower, an invasion across the Channel seemed to leave the Prime Minister cold. He waxed hot, however, in weekly presentations of his arguments for a Mediterranean assault and of his fears that the Channel tides would run red with the blood of American and British youth. Eventually he "hardened" (in his own phrase) to the Overlord enterprise and assured the Supreme Commander, "If you free our beautiful Paris by Christmas, I shall proclaim it the greatest military victory of all time." In late July the city's liberation was not more than weeks away.

Undaunted by this evidence of successful strategy, Churchill, who had transferred his opposition from Overlord to the Anvil landings on the South of France, argued still more vehemently against that auxiliary operation and Eisenhower's sponsorship of it. "Our new situation," wrote the General in *Crusade in Europe,* "brought up one of the longest-sustained arguments that I had with Prime Minister Churchill throughout the period of the war. This argument, beginning almost coincidentally with the break-through in late July, lasted throughout the first ten days of August." When Churchill finally acquiesced to the landings in the South of France, Eisenhower wrote:

Recently I had a telegram from the Prime Minister in which he seemed to be most enthusiastic about Anvil. When

I think of all the fighting and mental anguish I went through in order to preserve that operation, I don't know whether to sit down and laugh or to cry. In any event, I sent him a wire and told him that since he had now apparently adopted the newborn child it would grow quickly and lustily.

Thereafter, Churchill seems to have forgotten the Balkans, replacing his enthusiasm for them with a new conviction. The Allies had to reach Berlin before the Russians. In April 1945, he was insisting that Montgomery drive forward on the German capital. Again Eisenhower disagreed firmly. On April 15, less than four weeks before V-E day, he wrote: ". . . To plan an immediate effort against Berlin would be foolish in view of the relative situation of the Russians and ourselves at this moment." (The Russians were then in the Berlin suburbs and the Allies' forward spearheads one hundred miles away.) "We'd get all coiled up for something that in all probability would never come off. While true that we have seized a small bridgehead over the Elbe, it must be remembered that only our spearheads are up to that river; our center of gravity is well back of there."

Twelve days later he could report to Marshall: "The Prime Minister is finally waking up to one danger that I have been warning him about for some weeks, namely, the possibility that the Russians can reach Lübeck and the neck of the Danish peninsula ahead of us. I have done everything humanly possible to support Montgomery and to urge him to an early attack across the Elbe to Lübeck . . . I am hopeful that before you can receive this he will be advancing rapidly. I sent him a telegram today, pointing out again the urgent need for speed."

The Russians meanwhile were as hypnotized by Berlin as Churchill was, and, in their headlong race to get there first, they missed the chance to beat Montgomery to Lübeck and thus lost access to the North Sea. For a second time, the Prime Minister had seen Eisenhower's decisions justified by events. Within a few months, however, hindsight would arm Eisenhower's critics for an attack. Had he permitted an expedition into the Balkans, they said, those countries would not now be behind the Iron Curtain. Had he permitted Montgomery, who was closest to it, to advance on Berlin, the German capital would not be a beleaguered island in a Red sea.

To the critics, Eisenhower might easily have answered that a Balkans diversion would have crippled the liberation of France, and that concentration on Berlin would have left the northern flats of Germany open for a Red sweep to the North Sea and given the Russians a door on the Atlantic Ocean. Even so, he made no defense. Bickering over what might have been has always impressed Eisenhower as a futile occupation. In his "Victory Order of the Day" on May 8, he exhorted the troops:

Let us have no part in the profitless quarrels in which other men will inevitably engage as to what country, what service, won the European war. Every man, every woman, of every nation here represented has served according to his or her ability, and the efforts of each have contributed to the outcome. This we shall remember—and in doing so we shall be revering each honored grave, and be sending comfort to the loved ones of comrades who could not live to see this day.

Each soldier's mission had been the destruction of Hitler's armed power. That mission had been accomplished. Eisenhower was justly proud of the American part in it. "It is certain," he wrote George Marshall on April 27, 1945, "that the mass feeling of the three million American soldiers here is that they have done a remarkable job. The men remember the situation existing when we started shipping this army to Europe three years ago, and recall the respect, if not awe, in which we then held the German fighting prowess. They regard their accomplishments with great pride. This mass feeling is shared by officers as well as men. For a tremendous number of them, names such as Bradley, Spaatz, and Patton have become symbols. In the reputations of those men the mass sees its own deeds appreciated, even glorified."

Thus Eisenhower concluded the active phase of his Supreme Command. The war was over. For a time at least the free peoples of the world could look forward to the peace and the relaxation they all deserved.

Eisenhower had carried the burden of leadership with characteristic courage and good will. Typifying the spirit of America's strength, he held fast to his simple faith that stubborn devotion to a just cause assures success whatever the odds may be.

But now he, along with millions of others, was tired. He wanted only to get back to America and settle down with his family to the rest he felt he had earned.

CHAPTER SEVEN

THOUGH EISENHOWER looked forward to a long rest following V-E Day—he had hoped, in fact, to be able to retire from active life almost completely—the situation both in Europe and in the United States made this impossible. During the war, Eisenhower's duties were more in the nature of effecting international unity and teamwork rather than dealing simply in strategy and tactics. With the war over, the struggle for international co-operation continued. And Eisenhower very quickly recognized that his job had by no means ended with the cessation of hostilities.

For twenty years at least he has frequently quoted Woodrow Wilson's statement, "The highest and best form of efficiency is the spontaneous co-operation of a free people." This sentence is one of his fundamental axioms, just as freedom and responsibility are the two central concepts that invariably crop out in the substantial body of his letters and speeches dealing with unity in the squad, the nation, or in the community of nations. His central concern has, for many years, been to reconcile man's essential freedom, which permits him to go his private way unhindered, with society's need for order.

Possibly the problem of co-operation among men came to dominate his thinking and acting because of his own successful struggle in solving it. His personal convictions in this respect, however, are based on no philosophic certainty. There are many who write him off as just another man who has practical know-how in dealing with individuals and groups, and he himself derides any imputation that he is either a philosopher or an elucidator of the obscure. "All I do," he says repeatedly, "is belabor the obvious." What is most obvious to him today, as obvious as two plus two equals four, is that freedom can be preserved only by a constant exercise in co-operation. Isolation—social, political, or economic—leads inescapably to total enslavement. Only when men are joined can they remain free. The applications are innumerable; and the objective is always unity, national unity, international unity.

After the war, when Communism became a major threat to freedom, Eisenhower saw that a co-operative unity among the European nations, not arms or troops or money from America, was the key to their successful defense. At every opportunity, he argued for it. The very fact that multitudes were opposed to European unity, others completely indifferent to it, and only a relatively few actively interested in its development gave him all the more reason for speaking out early and in a forthright fashion on the creative stages of European defense. He was experienced in the difficulties that beset co-operative endeavor among men and nations. And he knew the length of time it takes to resolve them. He could point out to his staff that even under the pressures of war, speaking a common language, and engaged in the same profession of arms with like traditions and attitudes, the American and British staffs had wasted many precious months before they reached a working unity. At the same time, he could remind them that here at home unification of the various branches of the American Armed Forces was essential. Despite wartime evidence of the necessity for unification, it would require years of effort to overcome the prejudices against it. His own fight for it began a few weeks after V-E Day. On September 29, 1945, he wrote to George Marshall:

I am plagued by demands from all sorts of organizations at home to go on radio hookups or to appear at conventions and so on. In the case of most of them I can find a good excuse to say no, but once in a while I get involved in a way that forces me to write a short speech and send it home on a recording. Whenever I do have to talk I just keep hammering on two or three points, one of which is unification of the fighting services; another the need for universal training, and a third the need for international co-operation. In one that I forwarded today to the Herald Tribune *Forum, I also took occasion to outline in specific fashion the concrete policies we are trying to apply in Germany. As I have told everybody, from the President on down, many times, it will be most fortunate when the time comes that the Army can turn over German government to civilian officials.*

The installation of the civilian control in Germany was easier than the attainment of unification of the American air, naval, and ground forces. Throughout his entire term as Chief of Staff of the United States Army, from November 20, 1945 to February 7, 1948, Eisenhower fought continuously for unification. Once, just after his appointment had been approved by the Senate Military Affairs Committee, he presented the entire case in a long letter to Swede Hazlett. At the time he was at the Ashford General Hospital.

27 November 1945

Dear Swede:

This time your letter caught me in the hospital, flat on my back trying to ward off serious consequences from a very heavy cold and an attack of bronchitis.

With all that out of the way, I'll get down to the matter I want to discuss now. As you would guess, it is "unification." You reflect some of the fears I have heard voiced either in the press or verbally by other naval officers, namely, that some "swallowing up" process would inevitably follow upon any closer unification of the Services, at the top, than we now have. Frankly, I not only cannot understand how such a thing could come about—I am certain that no one wants it and I, for one, would battle it to the death. One brother does not devour another; a guard on a football team is equally important with the tackle!

The American public should understand that war has become a triphibious affair, and unless one laboriously picks out special circumstances, land, sea, and air in varying ratios are employed in every operation of war. The closest possible kind of association among the individuals of these three forces throughout their Service careers is mandatory. You must remember that for the past three and a half years I have not *been an infantry man; I have not been even a* ground *commander. I have had land, sea and air, and during that period I believe that my viewpoint has been as much naval and as much air as it has been ground. I do not mean that I've learned the techniques of sea and air; but if my headquarters had not had the sense to give as much weight to the technical advice of those two Services as in the case of ground, then our operation would have failed.*

Yet it was a laborious process at the beginning to weld all these three Services together and to convince each that its own characteristics, capabilities and welfare would be as influential in determining upon an operation as would those of the other two Services. Early conferences were carried on almost in the "cat-bulldog" atmosphere, each Service fighting for itself and its requirements and quite certain that no one else was concerned in them. This mutual suspicion and fear rapidly melted away and I think there is no question that G.H.Q., both in the Mediterranean and in Northwest Europe, was almost a model of unified, integrated and enthusiastic co-operation. But I believe that we should in time of peace so organize and train that a happy family can start operating in this fashion on the day we put it together, not after each Service finds by experience that the others regard it as a friend and part of the team rather than one of the enemies in the operation.

What I have said is not mere loose talk or even merely an impression. It is fact and I could give you a number of instances as specific illustrations. Moreover, the fault was not to be found exclusively with any one Service. However, all this is somewhat beside the point because everybody now agrees that in any war theater there should be one commander *and his authority should be so clearly established that there is no question as to his right to handle the three Services as he sees fit. The real point at issue is whether or not there would be any peacetime advantage in establishing by law a closer unification at the top.*

Now forget for a moment that you are a naval officer and regard yourself merely as a taxpayer. You are interested in national security and therefore in the armed forces of your country. You are entitled to some kind of presentation or explanation that would enable you to make a reasonable guess whether this whole subject is being properly treated by Congress or whether all of the fighting Services are being placed on a starvation basis and their efficiency reduced to former deplorable levels. Since war is a triphibious matter, how can you make any judgment on this matter at all—whether you are in private life or whether you are chairman of a congressional committee—unless the broad yearly program for all three Services is presented to you as a unit? *Do you not need to know whether ground forces have been provided to complement the navy and the air, and the navy both the others? If the members of each of these Services—and remember that service pride and esprit in each are equally strong—come to you* unilaterally *and plead for support, I am unable to see how you can get a balanced picture. Each of the Services will consider itself individually responsible for the safety of the nation and, if you are truly security minded, you will wind up with numbers of duplications which in the long run you cannot afford. The degree of autonomy that should be permitted to each Service so far as its own operations and its own affairs are concerned should not be lessened. But all of us must get into our heads that no one of these Services is complete within itself—that it needs the other two—and that since each is complementary to the other two, the whole program of preparation must be a balanced one. Added to this it is well to remember that the example of single command would have a great effect upon the second lieutenant and the ensign as well as upon all the men they command.*

It seems to me that such a system, also, will provide more easily for combined training and association of individuals through the years. On this subject I am almost a fanatic.

War is a matter of teamwork, and teamwork is not possible among people that are mutually suspicious. I will put it stronger than this; perfect teamwork can be achieved only *among friends.*

I had not heard that any other person had ever suggested a single uniform, which I did once, merely to illustrate the extent to which I believe we should all think of ourselves as one common family. I do not suggest what that uniform should be, and actually I think it is probably an impracticable suggestion, possibly even an unwise one, but if such a thing were adopted I personally would not care one whit what the color of the uniform should be. It could be blue, green, olive drab or sky blue and pink. On that point, however, I accept your suggestion and will not mention it again! [Swede had written: "Your (and MacArthur's) suggestion of one uniform was bad."]

One other thing I should like to make plain. I think I told you before of my admiration for Nimitz, based upon newspaper accounts and reports of friends, and many of the naval officers with whom I have come in contact in this war. Because it happens that argument on this subject has largely, to my astonishment, developed into an Army-Navy argument, I would very much like to see, if the thing ever comes about, a naval *officer designated as the first Chief of Staff to the Secretary of the Armed Forces. So far as I am concerned there is not the slightest bit of personal or Service consideration attached to the project. Until a few weeks ago every naval officer I had met was an enthusiastic supporter of the idea. I believed that there would be some argument on the matter, particularly in Congress, but I really thought that the great mass of Army and Navy officers were for the thing one hundred per cent.*

For myself, there is nothing I want so much as opportunity to retire. If this evening, as I lie here in bed, I could believe that when I got up I could get Mamie down here from her hospital and we could start out roaming the United States looking for the home we would like to live in the rest of our years, I would be up and on the go within twenty minutes. The job I am taking now represents nothing but straight duty. Naturally I will do it as well as I know how, but I do hope that when I get a chance to meet Nimitz and all the rest of the Navy files, I can convince them that no consideration of personal or Service ambition has a single thing to do with my personal views.

Cordially,

Ike

Although Eisenhower and Nimitz, joined by other leaders in the armed forces, strove to maintain throughout the discussions of unification an atmosphere free from prejudice and ax-grinding, frequently the controversy descended to personalities. Eisenhower himself was said to be interested chiefly in disbanding the Marine Corps. Navy and air men often became violent in their arguments, and their claims occasionally crossed the border of reason. The Army, with neither super-planes nor super-carriers, could do little more than lean on its Chief of Staff for support. As eloquently as he could, Eisenhower repeated the views he had expressed in his letter to Hazlett. But often his words fell on deaf ears. Nevertheless, unification became law July 26, 1947, when President Truman signed the enacting legislation. The *spirit* of unity, however, which meant more to Eisenhower than Congressional approval, was lost in the controversy that continued even after the law was passed.

As Chief of Staff, he faced many problems of which unification was only one. Beginning in November 1945, he oversaw the demobilization of the greatest fighting force ever assembled. It was an enormous task, as complex in many ways as bringing the Army together in the first place. Orderly at the outset and following a plan established more than a year before the shooting ended, the release of men was nevertheless far too slow for the people back home. Secretary of War Patterson's misinterpreted defenses and explanations of the demobilization program inflamed resentment among troop units in the Pacific, where he was visiting; subversive agents and ordinary Americans increased resentment to the point of mutiny; discipline began to crack around the world; in the United States, pressure to get the boys back home mounted to frenzy. Eisenhower, called to the capital to explain the whole business to Congress, was surrounded by anxious wives and mothers. In an address to the nation, on January 15, 1946, he repeated his explanation, assured men and families of an increase in the discharge rate, and ordered that troop demonstrations stop immediately. The general hysteria quickly died down. But the pressure groups did not quit.

No amount of persuasive argument could break them down. Each was organized to get the members' immediate relatives out of uniform—never mind those who had no group working for their release. Wives banded together to get all husbands home, *now*. Those whose kin had been medical or premedical students pointed to the shortage of doctors. Other groups found other factors that permitted them to make common cause. All of them bombarded their congressmen or Eisenhower with letters of appeal. The mail piled up in the Chief of Staff's office.

For a few days at the beginning of the year, Eisenhower tried to read each letter. It was a hopeless task. Thereafter, in the Correspondence Section, each plea was digested in a few sentences that included any unusual circumstances in the particular case, typed on long sheets, and brought to the Chief of Staff. Even then, his staff spent hours every day throughout January and February checking every case summary so that he—personally—could be sure of the facts.

Had the United States been in the same position after World War II that it occupied after World War I, Eisenhower would undoubtedly have stopped at nothing to disperse the Army as quickly as possible. But this time the postwar situation demanded a network of American bases extending over a far wider area than that covered simply in the theaters of war themselves. To maintain the occupation forces at a safe level, he had to strip the United States of all personnel not directly working on demobilization and recruiting, cut Panama and similar garrisons to the bone, and pull men out of rear areas where they were handling billions of dollars' worth of surplus property.

The administration of the occupied areas constituted not only a continuing drain on man power but served as a ready handle for complaints against the Army. Eisenhower believed that such administration was in no sense a military function. Repeatedly, while he was still in Europe, awaiting recall to the United States to succeed George Marshall as Chief of Staff, he reasoned with the President, congressional leaders, and presidential advisers against it. Except for the President, his listeners usually embarked on a counter-argument, saying that the character of the occupation administration did not matter so long as Eisenhower headed it. Some, like Sidney Hillman, were loud in their insistence that he should continue in Germany indefinitely and urged their views on President Truman, who, during the summer months, had accepted Marshall's suggestion that Eisenhower succeed him as Chief of Staff, and thus would not agree to a long extension of his European duty. Furthermore he saw eye to eye with Eisenhower that administration of the occupied areas should be turned over to civilians.

As the date of Eisenhower's return to the United States neared, it seemed evident that nothing would be done immediately about getting the Army out of civil government. Once more, in a letter to George Marshall on October 13, 1945, he expounded his arguments:

. . . the Government of Germany should, at the very earliest practicable moment, pass to a civilian organization. Long before the shooting was over in Europe, we, here, expressed this conviction and I have personally spoken about it to everyone from the President on down that I could get to listen. In spite of this I note frequent criticisms in the press at home about the stupidity of soldiers trying to run a civil government and, of even more importance from the War Department viewpoint, sometimes flatly stating that the Army is using the civil government of Germany to retain generals and to maintain strength.

While I realize that the present arrangement must continue until all four nations may agree that the civil functions here should be performed by a group council composed of civil rather than War Department representatives, yet I believe it would be a very fine thing for the War Department to make its own convictions on this point very clear indeed. I believe that our theme, constantly repeated, should be about as follows:

"The Army's true function in Central Europe is to provide for the United States that reserve of force and power that can insure, within our zone, the prompt enforcement of all laws and regulations prescribed by the Group Council, representing the four governments. Because Government in Germany had to begin from a situation of utter chaos, there was no one capable of initiating it except the Army. Nevertheless, the War Department consistently holds that the control and supervision of Germany, on a long-term basis, is a civilian

function, operating through German civil organizations which must be set up under policies we dictate and must be compelled to carry out the reforms we demand. Because of this conviction the American organization in Europe is so designed and so operated as to facilitate the transfer to civil authority of all governmental functions the instant that decision to that effect can be made by higher authority. Thereafter the occupational force will be strictly a reserve of force to be used when demanded."

The above, I believe, should be publicly stated over and over because, as I understand it, this is exactly the War Department conviction on the subject . . .

Congressional committees, visiting in my office, Secretary Ickes, Mr. Davies, Mr. Hillman, and others, have all professed themselves to be astonished to learn the Army actually wants *to turn over the governmental job to civilians as quickly as it is authorized to do so. One or two of them, such as Mr. Byron Price, thought he was going to have a real fight to convince* us *that civilians ought to do the job . . .*

As things now stand the Army comes in for criticism even from another point. This involves our selection of civilians to head up important Directorates in the Control Council machinery. You have probably noticed the vicious attacks made on Draper. Verbally, there have been even more bitter attacks made on others, some of whom gave up most remunerative jobs at home in order to do something that they considered a patriotic duty. As things now stand, the War Department, including forces here, receives violent criticism from everyone who may not happen to agree with, or personally to like, the individual selected.

What I should actually like to see is for the State Department to select and appoint now the man that they would expect, at the proper time, to serve as the American representative on the Group Control Council. That man should come over here, familiarize himself with the problems, and then go home to select from governmental circles and elsewhere the civilians he needs to round out his team or to replace people now here that he may not wish to keep. In this way he would instantly be able to take over whenever the four governments agree that the civil running of Germany should be turned over to civilian hands.

Less than two weeks later, on October 26, he repeated his views in a letter to the President, closing with a reminder that they had been in agreement on the matter when they discussed it at Frankfort on the Main, in July. In early 1946, however, the Army was constantly under attack for allegedly building a military autocracy in the occupied areas; and Eisenhower carried the burden of the defense.

Far more wearing than the desperate days of 1945 when he was sure that a decision would finally grow out of the confusion, the first quarter of 1946 was probably the roughest period of his professional career. Emotionalism, whose ultimate effect could not be foreseen, was destroying both American strength and prestige. There seemed to be nothing that he could do about it.

One evening in February, in the Secretary of War's office, when he was fagged out after a long conference on the critical shortage of men for assignment to Japan and Korea, a staff officer told him that public-opinion polls showed a growing satisfaction with the speed of demobilization. "You should be happy, sir," the officer added.

"I can be truly happy now only if I get completely out of official life," Eisenhower exploded. "Then, without inhibition or Government restraint, I could really shout from the house tops what we are doing to ourselves, our international influence and prestige."

But by the middle of March, the pressure groups had largely quieted down. Moreover, it was becoming increasingly apparent that Congress would extend Selective Service for at least two years more. The occupation government was acquiring a civilian tinge. Eisenhower, an incorrigible optimist, took up the reading of seed catalogs. At Fort Myer he planned to have his own vegetable garden for the first time in years. Like most Americans at the time, he had had his fill of war. He hoped to go fishing, as well as raise a garden, and perhaps even settle down on a ranch.

His own work, however, was far from over. The war had brought many changes to his life, not the least of which was fame. In the course of four years he had become a figure of world importance, and along with the glory he had to bear the burden of prominence and increased responsibility. The magnitude of this load is clearly indicated in the series of letters he wrote to his wartime chief of staff, "Beetle"

Smith, who was now serving as ambassador to Moscow.

August 30, 1946: "Mamie and I took a trip to Brazil, Panama, and Mexico which was one of the most enjoyable and at the same time one of the most tiring expeditions in which I have participated. The cordiality of the welcome not only bordered on the hysterical, but it was sustained throughout our stay in each city—five days in Rio, two days in Panama and three days in Mexico City. I was so worn out on my return that upon being overtaken by a slight attack of indigestion, I developed an illness that lasted for twenty-four hours, which was one of the most distressing things I have ever gone through. The doctor stayed with me constantly and, so far as I know, tried everything on me except the atomic bomb. My recovery was as quick as was my contraction of the trouble, and while I was left weak, I could still come to the office and go to work.

"Each day brings a succession of troubling and worrisome problems. There never seems to be a piece of good news. Such of these matters as are inescapable and inherent in current chaotic conditions, I can take in my stride. When they result from stupidity or negligence or complete lack of co-operation on the part of some of the other people with whom we have to deal, my patience and temper both give out. I will be more than delighted when the time comes that I can retire to a cabin somewhere and take it easy and let others worry about budgets and all the other things that are constantly on my desk."

February 13, 1947: "One of my worst problems is how to

decline a real flood of invitations that come from various associations, individuals, and patriotic bodies, all presenting altruistic or public-spirited purposes and all insisting that I could help them mightily by an appearance and a speech. Due to my very great desire to promote a few simple ideas in which I so earnestly believe, it is indeed difficult for me to say 'no,' except when I think I detect a mere desire on the part of a chairman or a secretary to use me for a little additional publicity for his meeting. The trouble is that in the vast percentage of cases I think the sponsors are really sincere and this of course awakens a desire on my part to help in my own feeble way. Nevertheless the whole thing is extremely wearing."

March 18, 1947: "Our problems here are many. The Budget is only one of them but this in itself is sufficient to keep most of the Department working frantically. It will be a great relief to me if General Marshall ever gets time enough where I can have with him a couple of long talks about our situation throughout the world. There is very obviously a definite limit to our resources. Concentration is indicated just as it is in war. I personally believe that it is not only vital that we decide upon the general plan we must follow but that we determine also the areas in which we can concentrate most advantageously. Beyond this it is equally important that the plan be so simple and on so high a moral plane that our people as a whole will understand its essentials and will earnestly and unitedly support it.

"Much of this of course is not my business but in writing

to an ambassador I feel I must discuss weighty subjects. Moreover, the working out of such a program affects everything that we do in the War Department. Beyond this, as a common citizen I have a tremendous concern in developments which appear so important to the future of our country."

April 18, 1947: "Frankly, this job is even more irritating and wearing than I had anticipated. We are still in the latter stages of destroying the greatest machine that the United States ever put together and at the same time trying to plan in orderly fashion to meet the needs of the moment as well as the longer range requirements of the future. It is an irksome task, particularly because, as always, the greatest enemies are prejudice, lack of understanding, and outright self-seeking. Moreover, there is no hope of getting a majority of our major problems settled in the reasonably measurable future and then settling down to the job of increasing efficiency through intensive training and education. I anticipate a period of at least three to four years of doubt, indecision, and practical bewilderment, but the struggle is to retain a sufficient sense of responsibility in high places so that out of it all we may emerge with something decent in the way of defense organizations. Of course, if it takes any such period as this, I hope I am not on this job to see the end, but if we are successful in getting Bradley [then in the Veterans Administration] back sometime during the coming year, there will always be a top-flight man to take over. Moreover, since you know me to be an incurable optimist, you will understand that I do not despair of a measurable degree of success. I think the thing that makes me angry is the particular character of so much of the opposition. So many things seem to be placed above the welfare of the country."

But as burdensome as his responsibilities as Chief of Staff became, his biggest problem at the time was a personal one, having nothing to do with military affairs. It was politics. Eisenhower, who in the summer of 1940 had wanted only to lead a regiment, was now being bombarded with requests to seek the presidential nomination. Again, the same sense of proportion that back in Fort Lewis had forbade him to cast himself in the role of Supreme Commander prevented him from taking these offers seriously. He had his duties as a soldier—and these duties, so far as he was concerned, had nothing to do with political office.

"There is no use my denying," he told his old neighbors in Abilene, on June 22, 1945, "that I'll fly to the moon, because no one has suggested it and I couldn't if I wanted to. The same goes for politics. I'm a soldier and I'm positive no one thinks of me as a politician."

One persistent questioner during a Pentagon press conference in the spring of 1946 trailed him into the corridor outside and insisted:

"Now, General, isn't there some circumstance, some very remote circumstance, that might induce you to get into politics?"

Stopping dead, Eisenhower spread his feet apart, shoved his hands in his pockets, and, emphasizing each syllable, said:

"Look, son. I cannot conceive of any circumstance that could drag out of me permission to consider me for any political post from dogcatcher to Grand High Supreme King of the Universe!" And he stalked off to his office.

By the summer of 1947, Eisenhower came to realize that the boomlets and booms were rooted in dead seriousness. Nevertheless, he continued adamant in his position. His greatest difficulty lay in phrasing his statements so that they could not be interpreted as a refusal of a national duty or a criticism of political life. On September 17, 1947, he wrote "Beetle" Smith:

I do not believe that you or I or anyone else has the right to state, categorically, that he will not *perform* any *duty that his country might demand of him. You did* not want *to become our ambassador to Moscow. There is no question in my mind that Nathan Hale accepted the order to serve as a spy with extreme reluctance and distaste. Nevertheless, he did so serve. Now in this matter of a political role the question naturally arises, "What circumstances could ever convince you or me that it was a* duty *to become a political candidate?" Certainly I do not see how anyone could obtain a conviction of duty from a deadlocked convention that should name him as a "compromise" selection after great portions of the delegates, representing equally large portions of the population, had failed to secure the naming of their own first choices. Under such circumstances I believe that instead of feeling a call to duty a man would have to consider himself merely a political expediency or political compromise. Consequently, as long as he should feel—as I do—that he does* not *want a political office and does* not *believe himself to be particularly suited for it, I think he would be perfectly within his rights to reject the suggestion.*

He continued through the succeeding four weeks to wrestle with his conscience. In letters to friends that were, in part at least, a self-searching of his own attitudes, he propounded all the arguments he could muster for an immediate and peremptory statement that he would not accept a presidential nomination if it were offered. Step by step, he clarified his position in his own mind. The fear remained that he could not escape the charge of dodging his duty, should he refuse absolutely. Gradually, however, he came to feel that this fear and the principle on which it was based had only an academic application in his case. One episode crystallized the feeling into certainty. On October 18, 1947, he wrote his brother Milton:

I think that nothing would please me more now than a chance to go to some isolated ranch in Texas at least a hundred miles from a railhead and stay there for one solid year. This gossip around the country that I am an aspirant for Republican nomination, or at least have a receptive mood with respect to the prospect, is beginning to damage my disposition—at times it becomes positively insulted.

Only this morning I noticed an account of a radio broad-

cast in which I was accused of having held a long and secret conference with Mr. [Henry] *Wallace and two of his colleagues, the alleged purpose of their visit being to persuade me to declare for the Democratic nomination with the purpose of ousting Mr. Truman.*

Not only is the entire story fantastic—the only one of the individuals mentioned in the story that I personally know was Mr. Wallace—but the implication that I had even countenanced people talking to me about a subject like this while I am still in the Army is very close to a challenge to a soldier's loyalty. The commentator did end his story with the conclusion that I had given Mr. Wallace no satisfaction because—according to him—I was personally hoping for the Republican nomination. The fact is that I have not even seen Mr. Wallace at a distance since he left the administration and I have never had a private talk with him in my life. Moreover, I have never mentioned the word "politics" to him, nor he to me.

The Wallace story was only the latest incident in a chain of gossip, rumor, and report about Eisenhower's secret political intentions and machinations. Completely unfounded, it ended his hesitation. He continued to Milton:

In any event, I merely cite these things to show you that I am getting very close to violating the one underlying principle that I have always believed to be binding on every American. This principle is that every citizen is required to do his duty for the country no matter what it may be. While

I am very clear in my own mind that no man since Washington has had any occasion to feel that it was his duty *to stand for or to accept political office, yet the principle remains valid. Because of this feeling I have so far been unwilling to say exactly what I'd like to say, but I do know this. I would never feel a sense of duty from a situation that saw a convention deadlocked for some days and which would finally, in desperation, turn to some name that might be a bit popular around the country, in the effort to drag a political and partisan organization out of the hole. That is exactly the kind of thing that Sherman answered so emphatically; under the same circumstances I would do the same.*

However, we are not children and we know that under the political party system of this country it would be certainly nothing less than a miracle if any group of delegates assembling for a convention felt such a terrific popular pressure behind them that they would instantly cease any effort to handle their work on a political basis and would respond to such a general sentiment. Since these are the only circumstances that I believe could impart a sense of duty to a normal human being, I come around again to the conclusion that by declining, in advance, to use words similar to Sherman's, I am merely punishing myself for adhering to a principle that has become certainly academic so far as any application to the present case is concerned.

I realize that a man should hold on to a sense of humor with sufficient strength to be able to laugh at the annoyances that I feel out of this whole thing. I believe that what irri-

tates me more than anything else is the veiled, sometimes open, charge that I am being dishonest. I am certain that ninety-nine per cent of the press representatives that I have ever met would accept instantly and without question my statement on any subject I could speak of in the world except only this one! It has become so much a practice in this country for political candidates to be coy and to try to preserve the illusion that "the office seeks the man, not the man the office" that it is difficult for anyone to carry conviction in his words when he is perfectly honest in saying that he wants nothing whatsoever to do with politics—well, I suppose there is no use pursuing this subject further. I doubt that in this letter I have told you anything that I haven't said to you often before. It is merely inspired by the fact that this morning I am a bit more irked than usual by the constant hammering.

On New Year's Eve, he told a friend: "I simply recoil from the thought that any American can say what he will or will not do for his country under circumstances of the unforeseeable future. But now the Wallace Third Party has taken me off the spot. The Republicans feel that anyone can win for them."

Many millions of people thought otherwise, and, before the middle of January, he was posing to his staff and his friends three questions:

"How can I say anything without violating my own sense of propriety?

"How can I decline something that has *not* been offered me?

"How can I answer men who are honestly convinced that I have a duty?"

Now it was no longer a simple choice between personal preference and duty. Had it been, Eisenhower would quickly have obeyed the latter. But duty had now become ambiguous. What, exactly, were his responsibilities as a citizen and as a leader? On January 12, 1947, Leonard V. Finder, publisher of the Manchester (N.H.) *Union-Leader,* wrote the following letter attempting to define what his and, he felt, the public's attitude was concerning Eisenhower's position.

Dear General Eisenhower:

As you know, a movement has been launched in New Hampshire to elect on March ninth a slate of delegates pledged to you. At the same time that this announcement was made public, the Manchester Evening Leader *came out with open endorsement of you as "The Best Man." For our actions, we have no apology, even though we are aware that you are not desirous of being involved in this political contest. We have acted consistent with our own belief, based upon what we regard as best for the welfare of the nation.*

Although I have sent Colonel Michaelis some of the newspapers and clippings indicative of our attitude—intending them actually for you—I am herewith enclosing a further tear sheet with our front-page editorial of last Friday. This is done to demonstrate how keenly we feel upon the subject, for I meant everything that was written therein.

While we appreciate that you are not anxious for political aspirations, we are equally confident that you will not resist or resent a genuine grass-roots movement. That is exactly what we have here in New Hampshire, because our plans were made without any inspiration from the National Draft Eisenhower League and without any other contact with politicians who might be seeking to advance their personal welfare.

As you once told me, no man should deny the will of the people in a matter such as this. All that we are attempting is to have the will of the people made so clear that it cannot be obviated by the usual politicians assembled in convention.

For nine days Eisenhower worried over his answer, writing draft after draft of a letter which he hoped would convey his attitude toward Finder's proposal. On Wednesday morning, January 22, he carried a finished version to his office from Fort Myer.

"It's long and laborious," he told his staff, "but it's the best I can do. And it's right, too. I still don't believe that many people want a soldier for President. I'm trying to be honest and realistic about it."

Now all he needed was the approval of his superior, James Forrestal, Secretary of Defense. Accordingly, he showed him the letter; after Forrestal suggested that he make a bow to politics as a profession, Eisenhower added the following sentence to the text: "Politics is a profession; a serious, complicated and, in its true sense, a noble one."

Contented at last, he returned to his office. The final version was typed and mailed, and a carbon was handed to the Public Information Division for release on January 23.

Your letter and editorial have been on my desk more than a week, while I pondered the reply merited by your obvious concern for the nation's welfare and, from a personal standpoint, by the honor you have done me. Months ago I thought that unqualified denial of political ambition would eliminate me from consideration in the coming campaign for the presidency, because that office has, since the days of Washington, historically and properly fallen only to aspirants. That some few would misinterpret or look for hidden meanings in my past expressions was expected and discounted, but my failure to convince thoughtful and earnest men, such as yourself, proves that I must make some amplification. This will necessarily partake of the laborious, due to the complexity of the factors that have influenced me to say no more than I have, but which dictate my decision that I am not available for and could not accept nomination to high political office.

I have heretofore refrained from making the bald statement that I would not accept nomination, although this has been my intention since the subject was first mentioned to me. This omission seems to have been a mistake, since it has inadvertently misled sincere and disinterested Americans. But my reticence stemmed from cogent reasons. The first was that such an expression would smack of effrontery. I had and have no desire to appear either as assuming that significant numbers of our people would actively interest themselves in me as a possible candidate, or to appear as lacking in respect and regard for the highest honor American citizens can confer upon one of their own body.

A second and even deeper reason was a persistent doubt that I could phrase a flat refusal without appearing to violate that concept of duty to country which calls upon every good citizen to place no limitations upon his readiness to serve in any designated capacity. On this point it is my conviction that, unless an individual feels some inner compulsion and special qualifications to enter the political arena—which I do not—a refusal to do so involves no violation of the highest standards of devotion to duty. It was only the possible misinterpretation of my attitude that caused me concern and so long as I could believe that mere denial of political ambition would prevent serious misunderstanding and misdirected effort, I was reluctant to say more. It would seem almost superfluous for me to add that as long as I live I shall hold myself in instant readiness to respond to any call by the government to military duty.

In full awareness then, and not in violation of my own sense of duty, I have developed the following conclusions, which are responsible for my negative decision.

It is my conviction that the necessary and wise subordination of the military to civil power will be best sustained, and our people will have greater confidence that it is so sustained, when lifelong professional soldiers, in the absence of some obvious and overriding reason, abstain from seeking high political office. This truth has a possible inverse application. I would regard it as unalloyed tragedy for our country if ever should come the day when military commanders might be selected with an eye to their future potentialities in the political field rather than exclusively upon judgment as to their military abilities.

Politics is a profession; a serious, complicated and, in its true sense, a noble one. In the American scene, I see no dearth of men fitted by training, talent, and integrity for national leadership. On the other hand, nothing in the international or domestic situation especially qualifies for the most important office in the world a man whose adult years have been spent in the country's military forces. At least this is true in my case.

I am deeply regretful if a too simple faith in the effectiveness of a plain denial has misled any considerable number concerning my intentions and so allowed them to spend time and effort under erroneous impressions. At the risk of appearing pompous, I must say that the honor paid me cannot fail to spur me, in future years, to work the more diligently for America, her youth, her veterans and all her citizens, and for the continuance of peace.

I trust that this rather lengthy explanation will convince you that my conclusions are not only sound but have been arrived at objectively and have not been unduly influenced by my own desires and convenience. In any event, my deci-

sion to remove myself completely from the political scene is definite and positive. I know you will not object to my making this letter public to inform all interested persons that I could not accept nomination even under the remote circumstances that it were tendered me.

To clinch the matter, the Public Information Division declared, in a short preface to the letter: ". . . General Eisenhower hopes through this means to inform every interested person or group that he is not in politics and that he would refuse nomination even if offered."

The day after the news broke, the Washington *Post* ran a Herblock cartoon of a disconsolate little "Mr. American Public," seated on a curbstone, head cupped in his hands, and staring through tears at the headlines lying in the street before him.

But however disconsolate the American public may have been at the news, it persisted in admiring its new hero, allowing him none of the relaxation he had earned and confronting him daily with the magnitude of his new responsibilities.

The quality of leadership which he had displayed as Supreme Commander impressed the American public enormously. And they were not easily to be disabused. They were convinced that at last they were in possession of a leader who epitomized their own hopes and ideals, who represented American independence and strength more than any other figure on the political horizon, and in whose inherent simplicity and fairness they could place their entire trust.

CHAPTER EIGHT

IN ADDITION TO the offers of political support with which Eisenhower was deluged during the latter part of his tour as Chief of Staff, he received scores of proposals from industry, finance, and publishing, which offered in many cases yearly salaries that were larger than the sum total of his personal income throughout his six years as a general officer. His Army pay had never made him rich. During the twenties and thirties, when he was a major and then a lieutenant colonel, he had watched his money carefully. Fortunately, his wife had always been an efficient manager with a superb knack for giving excellent parties at little cost. Thus Eisenhower never acquired the reputation of being niggardly, though he could hardly have afforded to be extravagant even if he had wanted to be. During his four years in the

Philippines, he was able to save a substantial part of his allowance from the Philippine government, but, even so, his extra earnings were hardly as great as those given a civilian employee whose firm sends him out of the country. For an Army family, however, every peso was a windfall.

When Lieutenant Colonel Dwight D. Eisenhower, aged forty-nine, graduate of West Point and three service schools, with a quarter century of successful work behind him, returned to the country from Manila in January 1940 with his wife and son, he was fairly well fixed for an Army field-grade officer. His bank account at Riggs in Washington would have provided a small, brick home—heavily mortgaged—on a fifty-foot lot in a nice suburb. But by March 1948, it had shrunk to little more than a few thousand dollars. Early that month a new automobile—a suitable town car, as the dealer described it, for the president of a great university—was delivered to Eisenhower's quarters at Fort Myer. The entire household, from the striker to the Douds, who were on a visit from Denver, as well as the Eisenhowers themselves, thronged out on the driveway and lawn to admire the car. For weeks there had been stories, emanating from the dealer's showrooms, that it would include the last word in fittings and gadgets; hydraulic-lift windows, three cigarette lighters, a reading lamp, and odds and ends never seen on an ordinary vehicle. The salesman had vowed that the agency would outdo itself on General Eisenhower's automobile.

Chief inspector and pusher of buttons was the man who a month before had been Chief of Staff of the United States

Army. Peering under the hood as a mechanic described the engine, bouncing on the cushions of the rear seat as the senior dealer expatiated on riding comfort, crouching behind the wheel as an agency partner explained the starter, shift, and switches on the dash, Eisenhower was in such a jolly mood that he would not be able to surpass it until he demonstrated to his grandson the operation of a new electric train.

The inspection and trial ended, he wrote a check in full payment for the new automobile. The balance left in his bank account was minute. He got up from the table, took Mrs. Eisenhower by the hand, and walked her to the door.

"Darling," he said, pointing at the car standing in the driveway, "there's the entire result of thirty-seven years' work since I caught the train out of Abilene."

Several of the offers that Eisenhower received during early 1947 offered salaries in the neighborhood of six figures. To a man who had for years been inclined to watch his half dollars, many of them seemed fantastic, and furthermore he was not interested in most of the positions that went with them. He had no trouble in declining them all; the intent to buy a name was too obvious in nearly every one.

But there was one offer that did attract him, and that was the presidency of Columbia University. The subject had first come up in the spring of 1946. At the time, however, he was not only reluctant to enter a field in which he was totally inexperienced, but he had no idea when his tour as Chief of Staff would end. On the other hand, he was preoccupied with many of the problems that a great university such as Columbia would help him solve. In late May 1946, he had written:

Any global war of the future will be ideological! Our most effective security step is to develop in every country, where there is any chance or opportunity, a democratic form of government to the extent that individualism rather than statism is the underlying concept. Russia, completely statist, sees this and is so anxious to spread communism that propaganda, money, agents, and, where countries are close to her borders, even force (are used) to see that Communism gets in the saddle. Without using the same methods, we should certainly be as determined in the attainment of our objective.

Although in this country we like to curse John Bull, yet Britain has done more than we to support countries that want to remain free. Britain is crumbling, has been ever since World War I, yet we gloat rather than get scared.

The underlying, important thing, therefore, is our national lack of understanding that we (our form of government) is under deadly, persistent, and constant attack! To lead others to democracy we must help actively, but more than this we must be an example of the worth *of democracy. Industrial power must be achieved, and increased productivity must follow or we are cutting our own throats.*

Our strength is a combination of:

1. Complete devotion to democracy, which means a faith in men as men (essentially religious concept) and practice of free enterprise. To maintain free enterprise we must police it but not *destroy it either by legislation or by class conflict.*

2. Industrial and economic strength.

3. Moral probity in all dealings.

4. Necessary military strength. This could be done at bearable costs if we understood the whole problem, because then we'd do it as a matter of pride and obligation, not on the basis of competing with industry.

All this demands a clear understanding of world issues and what we need to do at home to meet them. In the foreign field we have to select the areas in which we should and can help—and then go to work in every conceivable way! If this understanding were universal we'd have no strikes; capital and labor would easily solve their difficulties if both knew their very existence depended upon accord!

Later that year, as he was contemplating the probable effects of nationwide strikes, he became concerned that the tactics of some labor leaders might provoke legal restrictions on the rights of workingmen. His own sympathies were with the workers, among whom he had spent his childhood. Nonetheless he feared that some men in labor were so abusing freedom that their acts endangered it. Thus he added to his earlier note:

The only reason for freedom is to bring about a greater level of happiness and higher living standards to all *the people; and the free system deserves to survive only as long as it progresses in this direction. Everyone now recognizes that individual freedom can be lost in the operation of complex economies just as surely as it can under political dictatorship. The freedom must be real as well as legal—the unions have been right to fight for this. All these things are of interest to* all *the people; not just the employers and the workmen.*

The immediate problem has become—how to handle the striking right and privilege in key industries so as to avoid paralyzing the nation but so as to preserve the inherent rights of individuals . . .

The answer is easy in generalizations; it is difficult only in practical application, because, although everyone believes in co-operation (the single key) as a principle, no one is ready to abandon immediate advantage or position in practicing co-operation. Moral regeneration, revival of patriotism, clear realization that progress in any great segment is not possible without progress for the whole; all these are necessary.

In a free system, laws cannot fully *answer the problem; just as written agreements could not satisfactorily meet the requirements of Allied Command in war. We must produce a healthy economy, raise living standards for all, and preserve individual liberty.*

Going on to the problem of international relations, he said:

If our policy, as a matter of self-interest, is to help democracy (or any nation that wants to live by its own dictum as long as it pursues some form of democratic process) whenever we are specifically asked to do so, the policy with its reasons and purposes should be calmly explained to our people (and the world). Then, when asked for help, we could answer in timely fashion at half the cost and twice the effectiveness, without creating a furor. We should carry no chip on our shoulder—no special announcement would be necessary in any specific case. For God's sake, let's examine the world to determine:

A. *What nations deserve help.*
B. *Where is it practicable to give it.*
C. *Where will help do most to help us.*
D. *What should be its nature.*

Then let's do it in time, *without fuss, without saber rattling!*

On the fourth anniversary of victory in North Africa, May 12, 1947, he was even more emphatic on both national and international problems:

At home we have rising prices, labor troubles, housing shortages, and tax squabbles. Unless we find a formula which will stabilize the price structure we are due for most serious times.

Abroad there are so many nations needing *our help that the whole job seems appalling, even though it is clear that help to some of them is in our own interest.*

Great Britain, France, Italy, Greece, and Turkey are possibly foremost—although Germany and Austria likewise present situations that can grow most serious if we do not take positive and intelligent action. I personally believe that the best thing we could now do is to post five billion to the credit of the Secretary of State [George C. Marshall] *and tell him to use it to support democratic movement wherever our vital interests indicate. Money should be used to promote possibilities of self-sustaining economies;* not *merely to prevent immediate starvation.*

For the moment Britain's need is not money—but it needs food and, far more important, comprehensive assistance in getting its economy in working order. She is our greatest natural friend; we must *get her healthy.*

France somewhat the same, but more critical because of the Communist strength. Italy even more so! Time in these two countries is of the utmost importance. No use to save Greece and Turkey from Communism if these two should go!

All over the world (including South America), the story is the same though varying in intensity as to time and in critical importance to us. *The next two years should establish the pattern. If it is unfavorable to us, the result will be partly our own fault, but wholly black in the implications for the future.*

Increasingly as postwar tensions mounted, Eisenhower came to think more and more deeply about his global responsibilities. Back in the twenties he had been willing to accept Fox Conner's prophecies concerning a succession of world wars, but now that he himself was in a position to help avert such a catastrophe, he was determined to do everything within his power to understand the issues involved.

Accordingly in the spring of 1947, he made his decision to

go to Columbia, and, in a letter to "Beetle" Smith written on July 3, said:

. . . you can well imagine that it was a difficult decision for me. It was almost the first decision I ever had to make in my life that was directly concerned with myself. Of course I chose, thirty-six years ago, to go to West Point but that was not a decision; it was an instinctive desire that I followed persistently until I had attained it. Since that moment every problem with which I have had to wrestle has involved primarily a task or mission or a difficulty of some objective kind. In this one I had to struggle against every instinct I had. Moreover, I encountered the conviction of my friends that acceptance was a duty. As you know, I loathe the prospect of living in a big city—possibly a throwback to my rural boyhood. Next, I wanted to lead, after leaving this post, a semi-leisurely existence with enough to do to keep me occupied but without any feeling of tremendous compulsion driving me to long hours and to continuous work weeks. I think my real dream was to get a small college of an undergraduate character somewhere in the Virginia or Pennsylvania area or possibly even in the Northwest and to live quietly with Mamie in that kind of an atmosphere. Under such conditions I felt that I could write or not, just as I chose. I have given up all such dreams for the moment.

Much earlier in his career, in 1939 when he was still in the Philippines, his brother Milton had been faced with a strikingly similar dilemma. Uncertain whether to remain in the Government where he was with the Department of Agriculture, or accept a deanship at Pennsylvania State College, he wrote asking his brother's advice. Eisenhower's reply anticipated many of the answers to questions that he himself was to face eight years later:

I am quoting a sentence from your letter. "Finally, I am not certain that I would be entirely happy in work that lacked the rigorous demands on many fronts that I encounter here."

I feel competent to enter a discussion on this point because of similiar feelings of my own in the past, and some reflection on the results of my own decisions, that were based upon those feelings. The human machine wears out, although none of us ever applies this inescapable law to his own case. Deterioration and destruction are familiar phenomena, but the mind recoils from personal application of the logical conclusion. Signs of deterioration appear, just as they do in an automobile, in accordance with the speed of use. By tradition when we speak of "burning up the road" we think of strong drink, weak women and raucous singing. Actually the speed that is most dangerous to the human is the speed that is involved in driving, continuous, mental endeavor! *Men of ability in the government service see so much to be done, they create or have created for them so many jobs that lazier men like to shunt from their own shoulders (except of course when it comes to collecting the glory for recognized accomplishment) that gradually the victim, which word I use advisedly, loses his sense of values, and with this needful governor failing him, he applies his mind, consciously and unconsciously, day and night, to important and intricate problems that march up ceaselessly, one after the other, for consideration.*

In our younger days this is fine—we like it—we know with certainty that we are important to the organization we serve —and we thrive on the completion of each job, done to the full satisfaction of those around and above us. It can likewise be done and enjoyed by age with no great damage, but only where the conditions of service are such as to encourage, even force, increasing periods of enjoyable relaxation. To pursue further the automobile analogy; an old car must go for complete overhaul more frequently than the new one!

Most professional careers, even including the military, so arrange themselves that increasing opportunity to slow up in personal effort, to use the fruits of other men's work in arriving at decisions and judgments, comes with advancing years. A disadvantage that I've always suspected to exist in your present job is that this general rule does not apply. Secretaries and assistant secretaries will continue to come and go —and the able, conscientious bureau director, capable of taking on his own shoulders the thousand and one recurring administrative, co-ordinating and miscellaneous jobs will be scarce as ever. In other words, you, because of your nature and your recognized abilities, will be on a steady, swift grind until you've definitely damaged your own capacity for enjoying life. When tires blow out or pistons freeze, the car is no good to anyone—but these things are more readily repaired than a shattered nervous system or a confirmed routine of activity that finally cannot be broken except at the acute distress and damage of the individual. When this occurs real unhappiness results—for only a man that is happy in his work can be happy in his home and with his friends. Which, incidentally, leads to the observation that Helen, in collaborating with you in solving your present problem, should do so with the purpose of insuring the suitability, congeniality and interest of your life-work.

All this to pose one single proposition! My conception of a worth-while college dean is a man that, as years go by, becomes a guide and inspiration to our youth, not through feverish activity and solution of involved administrative problems, but through the ripened viewpoint from which he sees youth's questions, and the high average of wisdom and leadership he uses in helping them solve their problems. His value derives from character, knowledge and personality—not from ceaseless expenditure of nervous energy. Of course I realize that in entering upon a new post of this kind, a season of intensive effort would be necessary. But if the picture presented in this paragraph is reasonably accurate, the new job would appear to be one in which the demands conform closely to the proper output of ripening ability. In your present position, I feel, this characteristic is lacking, and you are in danger of becoming only an extremely useful tool! In other words, do we not have here a prospect for development, as opposed to possible stagnation?

CHAPTER EIGHT

In July 1947, Eisenhower, in a letter to his friend Swede Hazlett, echoed many of the arguments concerning Milton's deanship when he spoke of his acceptance of the Columbia presidency.

There are dozens of different considerations that finally influenced me to say "yes" to the Columbia trustees. One of these considerations was their clear understanding of the point that I would never really separate myself from the uniformed services of the country. I explained to them carefully that I have lived thirty-six years with one idea and for one purpose and that as a result I had absorbed several simple concepts that would remain with me until the end of my days. From my viewpoint, going to Columbia is merely to change the location of my headquarters; perhaps it would be more accurate to say that I am changing the method by which I will continue to strive for the same goals.

I believe fanatically in the American form of democracy —a system that recognizes and protects the rights of the individual and that ascribes to the individual a dignity accruing to him because of his creation in the image of a supreme being and which rests upon the conviction that only through a system of free enterprise can this type of democracy be preserved. Beyond this I believe that world order can be established only by the practice of true co-operation among the sovereign nations and that American leadership toward this goal depends upon her strength—her strength of will, her moral, social, and economic strength and, until an effec-

tive world order is achieved, upon her military strength. It is these simple concepts that I will take to Columbia. If by living them and preaching them I can do some good, I will hope to stay on indefinitely.

I did not mean suddenly to become pontifical—I have merely been struggling to get over to you something of my basic reasons for deciding to undertake that job when the time comes that the President feels I may be released here.

Eisenhower accepted the presidency, with a clear understanding that if at the end of his first year he was not convinced of his fitness for the post he would resign. With this in mind, he and Mamie arrived at 60 Morningside Drive, the President's House on the Columbia campus, at 4:30 the afternoon of Sunday, May 2, 1948.

Eisenhower was at his desk at 8:15 the following morning. For an hour and a half he worked over his mail. Then followed a succession of forty-five minute interviews with Robert Harron, Columbia public information director, Harry Carman, dean of Columbia College, Frederick Coykendall, chairman of the Columbia trustees, accompanied by M. Hartley Dodge, the clerk of the Board, and Albert Jacobs, provost of Columbia University. At 1:30 he lunched with Dr. Frank D. Fackenthal, for more than two years acting president of the University, and the trustees. From 3:15 to 3:30 he held a press conference in the Faculty Club and at 4:00 attended an hour-long trustees' meeting in Lowe Library.

That ended, the trustees walked across the rotunda to the

president's office and talked informally for better than an hour. When the last trustee left, Eisenhower read through the letters he had dictated earlier in the day, signed them, read some mail that had arrived during his conferences, and arrived home after a four-minute walk down 116th Street. He was back in 60 Morningside at 7:15. And in so doing, he had set a pattern that he would follow closely for the next thirty-two months.

Within his first two weeks, he had long talks with eleven of the University's deans and directors and half a dozen key professors in various institutes; attended a trustees' dinner, a luncheon of the International Committee for Mental Hygiene; became a trustee of the Carnegie Endowment for International Peace; spoke before the New York State Chamber of Commerce; made a recording of his D-Day message to the troops; attended an hour's conference on alleged racial discrimination on the campus; accepted three invitations to speak; and signed more than three thousand prepared answers to correspondents, as well as handling his own personal mail and keeping thirty-two office appointments other than those with the administrative and faculty staff. From the outset, at Columbia, he found none of the leisure of an elm-shaded campus.

Despite the crowded hours, Eisenhower was able to start work on one of his favorite projects. Even since the winter months of 1944, he had thought seriously about the need for a scientific study of America's man-power resources. At that time the Allied armies were crowding toward the Rhine. A critical man-power shortage made impossible the continuance of rotation for battle-worn veterans, jeopardizing troop morale, and weakened the Allied line. Yet, at the same time, many tens of thousands of men, physically sound, were in hospitals suffering from psychoneuroses and other mental ailments or were assigned to duty in the United States as unfit for overseas service. "They were essentially afraid of life," Eisenhower later said of them, "but they believed they were afraid of death."

During his second day in the president's office, he discussed the subject at luncheon with Philip Young, dean of Columbia's Graduate School of Business, and Dr. Eli Ginzberg, a brilliant young member of the faculty. Out of their discussion came the decision to start an extensive study on the Conservation of Human Resources.

The New York metropolitan area provided a unique research laboratory. The medical records of hundreds of thousands of veterans living there were available. Clinical studies and case histories could be developed more easily in New York than in any other section of the country. Out of surveys and studies by experts in the psychological, social, and industrial fields, might come conclusions, counsel, possibly even solutions for the psychoses and neuroses of the industrial age.

A few weeks after the luncheon meeting, Columbia opened an office in the Graduate School of Business building and began accumulating materials for the study. Since no university had ventured into this field, progress was slow. Young and Ginzberg had many other duties and commitments, but Eisenhower continued patiently to push the project. His own time was burdened with interruptions of all sorts, academic, military, and civic. It was not until the opening of the 1951–52 school year that the program for the Conservation of Human Resources reached the status he had hoped for in May of 1948.

The first major interruption after Eisenhower began work at Columbia was a renewal of political pressures, this time that he accept the Democratic nomination. By middle June, as many as four hundred letters arrived in one mail. Senators and congressmen, almost daily, phoned for appointments. None would take the January letter as Eisenhower's final word, and another statement had to be issued by Robert Harron's office at Columbia University.

5 July 1948

MEMORANDUM FOR MR. HARRON
DIRECTOR OF PUBLIC INFORMATION
COLUMBIA UNIVERSITY

I know that your office has for some days been overburdened with innumerable queries concerning my intentions in regard to the current political situation. My decisions and earnest conviction concerning possible personal connection with this year's political contest were given to the public several months ago, but it now appears that there has arisen a question as to whether or not I have changed my position. Pro-

foundly touched by the renewed suggestion that I could satisfactorily fill high public office, my views with respect to my proper course of duty are still identical with those presented in the letter I wrote on January 23, 1948.

In response to any further queries as to my course of action during the foreseeable future, and in order that there may be no possible room for doubt in the mind of any interested American, will you please invite attention to the firm purposes expressed in my January letter and quote the following as coming personally from me.

> *"I shall continue, subject to the pleasure of the University Trustees, to perform the important duties I have undertaken as President of Columbia. I will not, at this time, identify myself with any political party, and could not accept nomination for any public office or participate in partisan political contest.*
>
> *"This implies no intention of maintaining silence on any issue of importance to the country on which I may feel qualified to express an opinion."*
>
> *Dwight D. Eisenhower*

Thus ended political interference—at least for a while. The July fifth statement left no further room for doubt. Eisenhower was out of the presidential picture completely and determined to "perform the important duties [he had] undertaken as President of Columbia University." Thereafter, he devoted all his energies to the campus. After a brief trip to Denver during the summer, he returned to New York and began to learn as much as he could about the physical, financial, and academic structure of a university whose normal enrollment exceeded twenty-five thousand students, whose faculty numbered more than three thousand, whose maintenance staff was almost four thousand, and whose annual budget exceeded eighteen million dollars.

By the time of his formal inauguration on October 12, he was convinced that he was ready for the job. In his address that day, he spoke of his hopes that the University would be characterized by:

"First, an undergraduate body of men and women, schooled in the broad expanse of human knowledge and humble in their heritage—resolute that they shall pass both on with some increase. From among them will come scholars, executives, statesmen. But Columbia shall count it failure, whatever their success, if they are not all their lives a leaven of better citizenship.

"Second, a graduate body of men and women who, each in his own field, shall advance frontiers of knowledge and use the techniques of science in the service of humanity. From among them will come skilled surgeons, engineers, lawyers and administrators, great leaders in every profession and science. But again, we shall count it failure, if they, by specialization, become blinded to human values and so ignore their fundamental duty as citizens.

"Third, Columbia University will be: a dynamic institution as a whole, dedicated to learning and research and to

effective co-operation with all other free institutions which will aid in the preservation and strengthening of human dignity and happiness. Our way of life and our university are the flowering of centuries of effort and thought. Men of the ancient world—in Jerusalem and Athens and Rome; men of all epochs, all regions, and all faiths have contributed to the ideals and ideas that animate our thinking. Columbia University is, and shall continue, both heir of that past and a pioneer in its future increase."

For the first time since he had left Abilene, Eisenhower was engaged in civilian pursuits. But the transition was hardly striking. Business clothes suited him well and so did his new occupation. His duties depended chiefly upon his powers to organize a vast and complicated enterprise of many diverse interests—a giant among universities, and one whose great vitality was on the point of exhaustion. It needed direction badly after many years of one man rule. It had grown enormously during the early part of the century, under the guidance of Nicholas Murray Butler. But in 1947 the momentum acquired during Butler's administration had begun to diminish. The school needed new life.

In return for the vitality that Eisenhower brought Columbia, he received among other things an invaluable opportunity to express himself on many matters which his military status had forbidden him to discuss openly. During his Columbia period, he spoke freely about many of the urgent problems that had been on his mind for years, and in his public statements he committed himself without hesitation to the principles which had guided his career from its inception. He spoke about the need for hard work in settling international differences and of the necessity for enlightened self-interest in domestic matters. He urged that America maintain firm ties with the Continent and that at home it learn to trust its people to seek their own welfare according to their own interests and capacities.

CHAPTER NINE

EISENHOWER had begun to feel the impositions of fame almost from the day he returned to the United States. Despite his rise to world prominence, he was unused to being a public figure; nevertheless, during his first year at Columbia he averaged an important talk every other day. Thereafter, the pace slackened only slightly.

He brought little practice in oratory to the speaker's platform, beyond what he had acquired in elocution class back in Abilene. Although naturally earnest and evidently sincere, he never achieved either the grand manner or the striking artifices of the oratorical great. He spoke usually as if he were addressing a group gathered informally for a friendly discussion. The only trick he knew was the use of a humorous anecdote at the beginning to gain the audience's attention. He seemed to have only three such stories, and many of his listeners had heard him speak often and knew them well. Fortunately for them, he frequently abandoned the curtain raiser and plunged directly into his subject.

One story concerned a paratrooper to whom Eisenhower had given a ride in his plane when he was returning to the United States for the celebrations following V-E Day in June 1945. The young soldier, according to the General, was completely relaxed all the way across the Atlantic, buried in comic books, showing no interest in the plane, the sky, or the sea. But as the ship descended over the National Airport in Washington, he became excited, running from one window to another. Finally, he thrust his head over the General's shoulder, peering out. Eisenhower, a little surprised at his evident agitation, asked: "You've been in a plane before, haven't you, son?" "Yes, sir," shot back the paratrooper, "seventeen times, but this is the first time I've ever landed!"

More times than the paratrooper had not landed, Eisenhower told the story, until he himself prefixed it with the request that since most of the audience had already heard it half a dozen times would they delay their yawns until he had reached his punch line.

Apart from this initial handicap, Eisenhower's speeches carried great conviction; so much so that the New York luncheon and dinner circuit, accustomed to speakers whose wares were usually a long collection of humorous stories or a grim statistical survey of things going to ruin, warmed to him immediately. His listeners were frequently amazed that a professional soldier could speak so fluently on subjects so far afield from war.

"Emphasis on the obvious rather than elucidation of the obscure makes an Eisenhower talk something unique for a New York audience," said a Columbia trustee, commenting on the General's fluency.

"The family, church, and school as the foundation of American society," he continued, "freedom, co-operation, unity as its political core, the Mosaic Decalogue and the Sermon on the Mount as the source of its spiritual strength—that sort of talk the people in this city seldom hear."

One of his favorite topics was, of course, Columbia. His major purpose, as he had said in his inaugural address, was to make it a dynamic institution, "dedicated to learning and research and to effective co-operation with all other free institutions for the preservation and strengthening of human dignity and happiness."

Just as often, however, he chose subjects of a somewhat broader nature—subjects proceeding from those very questions which had originally impelled him to accept the university appointment. These were the topics of national and international significance which had been troubling him for years—statism, Communism, the rights and privileges of labor and capital, the function of government in a free society, the prospects of peace, the likelihood of war. His conclusions in these matters generally derived from the spirit of enlightened individualism combined with co-operative endeavor that he had had since childhood. Repeatedly, he emphasized these themes, applying them whenever he had the chance.

Once in a Labor Day speech given in 1949, he had an opportunity to state his bitter opposition to the Marxist fallacy that capital and labor are, by the nature of their respective positions, in constant opposition. He disagreed heartily with this proposition, saying:

"A little more than a century ago the Communist Manifesto *of Karl Marx was published, preaching the falsehood of an inescapable class warfare that would continue within such a society as ours until by violence the workers erased all traces of traditional government. If Marx were right, this day should be, in all our great country, an annually recurring provocation to riot, physical strife and civil disorder. The factual evidence of his blunder is so clear that it ought not to require emphasis.*

"Nevertheless, with a full century of contrary proof in our possession and despite our demonstrated capacity for cooperative teamwork, some among us seem to accept the shibboleth of an unbridgeable gap between those who hire and those who are employed. We miserably fail to challenge the lie that what is good for management is necessarily bad for labor; that for one side to profit, the other must be depressed. Such distorted doctrine is false and foreign to the American scene, where common ideals and purpose permit us a common approach toward the common good. It must be

combated at every turn by both clear word and effective deed.

". . . the American system in line with its principles can and does, by governmental action, prevent or correct abuses springing from the unregulated practice of a private economy. In specific cases local governments have, with almost unanimous approval, provided needed public services so that extraordinary power over all citizens of the community might not fall into the hands of the few. In all cases we expect the government to be forehanded in establishing the rules that will preserve a practical equality in opportunity.

"We, in turn, carefully watch the government—especially the ever-expanding federal government—to see that in performing the functions obviously falling within governmental responsibility, it does not interfere more than is necessary in our daily lives. We instinctively have greater faith in the counterbalancing effect of many social, philosophic and economic forces than in arbitrary law. We will not accord to the central government unlimited authority, any more than we will bow our necks to the dictates of the uninhibited seekers after personal power in finance, labor or any other field.

"Extremists hope that we lack the stubborn courage, the stamina and the intelligent faith required to sustain the progress of the attack. By appeals to immediate and specialized selfish advantage, they would blind us to the enduring truth that no part of our society may prosper permanently except as the whole of America shall prosper. They use the cloying effect of subsidy as well as the illusory promise of an un-

earned and indolent existence to win our acceptance of their direction over our lives. They believe that the intricate interdependencies of our highly industrialized economy will drive us to desert principles in favor of expediencies—particularly the expediency of governmental intervention.

"Thus far the record belies their hopes. Consider the abundance of courage and faith, manifested thousands of times each year in union meetings when workingmen penetrate the ideological complexities, parliamentary maneuvers [and] entangled plottings of Communist agitators, exposing and defeating them. Consider also the many thousands of times each year in meetings of management when businessmen—though primarily charged with concern for cost, production, distribution and profit—subordinate those material things to increasing the welfare of their employees. Were it not for those, in both management and labor, who fight and work to keep us from the ditches on the right and left, then indeed this day would be a symbol of class warfare, and the city of St. Louis—and every other great industrial city—would be a battleground for what Marx called the proletariat.

"But, in public places, soon only the specious promises of the extreme right and the extreme left may make themselves heard. The truth can be lost if the peddlers of lies go unchallenged. To defeat them in their campaign of falsehood, we must first destroy their stock in trade—the shibboleth of an irreconcilable difference between those who manage and those who operate.

"Marx appealed to the self-pity, the justifiable resentments

of the proletariat in the Europe of his day. He could not imagine a great nation in which there is no proletariat, *in which labor is the middle class that he so much despised and hated. He could not foresee that millions of plain people would, in two World Wars, stake all they possessed in defense of ideas and ideals that were hardly more than shadowy dreams to most Europeans of a century ago. He could not imagine that one day the grave of an unidentified soldier would become a symbol of our dedication to political, economic and social freedom . . .*

"You realize that the interests of labor and management in most situations are identical. Differences are centered almost exclusively in the annual bargaining conferences. But even here the true differences are far more apparent than they are real. For intelligent management certainly recognizes the need for maximum income to workers, consistent with reasonable return on investment. With equal clarity, labor cannot fail to recognize the need for increasing amounts of risk capital to provide jobs for our constantly growing population. And—make no mistake about it—no group in our country is more firmly dedicated to the retention and development of our system of private competitive enterprise than is American labor."

Eisenhower's conception of the American workingman not as a member of the proletariat but of the middle class is based upon his own, practical experience. He knows the country's workingmen as intimately as he knows his own background and he respects their independence as firmly as he does his own. When they are strong and bound together in productive, enlightened unions they have nothing to fear from the threat of poverty or dispossession as Marx insisted. If they and industry can work together efficiently, recognizing each other's needs and privileges, they need not depend upon the federal government for support. They are sufficiently strong by themselves.

As a civilian, Eisenhower was happy to express his opinions freely and openly on such subjects and he seldom missed an opportunity to do so. He abhorred the reactionaries of the extreme right as profoundly as those of the far left. He himself held firmly to a middle-of-the-road position, accepting change when it seemed proper but rejecting irresponsible bureaucratic meddling with existing institutions as long as they remained valuable. In a speech before the American Bar Association in the fall of 1949, he said: "The central position . . . is the truly creative area within which we may obtain agreement for constructive social action, compatible with basic American principles, and with the just aspirations of every sincere American. It is the area in which are rooted the hopes and allegiance of the vast majority of our people."

It was just this middle-of-the-road policy, allowing for "constructive social action" within the limits of America's present system, that Eisenhower hoped to foster in his work at Columbia. Rather than encourage drastic revisions of present American institutions, he set out to confirm and clarify the principles that already existed. One of his favorite projects was the education for citizenship program; another was the nutrition study, established to rectify some of the remediable food and diet deficiencies throughout the world; a third was a research into the causes of war. Each of these proposals, and several others like them, required many long meetings to thrash out their details and overcome the inertia that followed one-man rule at Columbia.

But just when new life and activity had begun to flow through the campus, Eisenhower was called to Washington, as senior adviser to James Forrestal, first Secretary of Defense. Through four hectic months, commuting between Washington and New York, speaking at civic functions and academic gatherings, sitting in on meetings that weighed security elements in the national budget or the appropriations for departments in Columbia University, Eisenhower undertook to do two killing jobs simultaneously.

On February 28, 1949, he flew from Washington, where he had just finished two weeks of Joint Chiefs of Staff sessions, to Chicago, where he was to open the American Red Cross drive. In that city, he attended two Columbia University luncheons and spoke at the Red Cross meeting, at two Columbia alumni meetings, and before the high-school class taught by a Columbia graduate who had given half a month's pay to her alma mater. On March 2, flying back to Washington for another round of meetings and warned in flight by a staff member that he could not maintain his present pace for long, Eisenhower was buoyantly confident that he could finish off his national defense chores in three weeks and get back to full-time work at Columbia. Three weeks later to the day, he was flown in President Truman's personal plane to the Naval Hospital at Key West. Physical exhaustion two days earlier had been the penalty for too much attention to duty.

Not until May 11 was he in shape for a renewal of the Washington meetings, and it was May 17 before he returned to his Columbia duties. In his first public speech, the address at the 195th Commencement Exercises of the University on June 1, he hinted of his longing for a quieter life. At the start of the talk, he said:

"When Columbia's first graduating class was awarded its degrees, the pace and tempo of the human world had changed little from the days of the Caesars and the Pharaohs. Life then, as viewed from our observation post two hundred years later, had in it more of leisure and less of strain; more of meditation and less of hysteria; more of faith and confidence and less of doubt and fear."

By the end of his first academic year, Eisenhower felt that he understood Columbia's structure and its needs. He knew too that in order to satisfy these needs he would have to participate in the school's fund-raising activities—a pursuit which ill suited his talents and inclinations. He balked absolutely at every suggestion of tin-cup activity; under no circumstances would he bluntly ask any individual for a contribution, large or small. An old friend on June 10, 1949, had written him: "Will you forgive me if I intrude a personal note? You do not need my advice or counsel. I cannot refrain, however, from speaking out. I do hope that you will not become too much engrossed in that part of your executive duty, as President of this great University, which will possibly absorb all of your energies in administrative detail. Even the solicitation of funds, important as it is, you should delegate. There are others who can relieve you, of that I am sure. My point is that your energies are far too valuable, and your abilities are too unique to be expended in that way."

There were other reasons too for his inability to become a professional solicitor. For one thing, his name, position, prestige—accidentals extraneous to the merits of the Columbia case—might be interpreted by the prospect as a pistol at his head. For another, Eisenhower simply did not have it in him to raise funds. Constitutionally averse to begging, however high-sounding the euphemism applied to it, he was almost certainly the poorest excuse for a fund-raising college president in the country; and he frankly admitted his inadequacy. Nevertheless, he was always ready to present the merits of Columbia University whenever the occasion arose. By June of 1949, he was confident that he had a case that merited a generous response.

He had no need of a prospect list drawn up by professional fund-raisers. His roster of friends comprised some of the wealthiest and, he hoped, most generous givers in America. Those in New York City, unfortunately, had school loyalties, affiliations with charitable enterprises, or philanthropic commitments, of many years' standing that militated against either an early or a substantial interest in Columbia University. Given enough time, however, he was sure that he could win their support. But in the next year or two, he had to break the log jam. Continued stagnation would result in raids on the faculty by schools with money enough to lure them away, deterioration in buildings, decrease in enrollment—all the penalties of standing still.

He decided to approach friends in Texas, and on June 27, 1949, wrote to one of them:

As I told you, I am not seeking from you direct financial help for Columbia. I am well aware of, and heartily endorse, the many altruistic ventures that have engaged your attention. I am equally aware of the splendid purposes you have had in mind in establishing the Foundation. Moreover, my particular philosophy of democracy insists upon local and community responsibility as the basis for successful political and social organization. I would be the last to urge the neglect of local problems.

On the other hand, I think that none of us can forget that there must be established and maintained a common understanding of the American system, common appreciation of its values, and common devotion to its fundamental purposes. . . .

For many years, and particularly during and immediately after the war, I became greatly concerned with what seemed to me to be a progressive change in basic thinking—possibly I mean aspirations—in our country. The ambitions of our pio-

neering ancestors, as I understand them, were to secure opportunity for social, economic, and political betterment under a system that insured individual freedom and complete equality before the law, with no domination by governmental bodies other than that necessary to make certain that liberty did not degenerate into license—in other words, that no individual, while insisting upon his own rights, should trespass upon equal rights of others. Now, many of us seem to want only a powerful and beneficent central government which will insure us nice jobs during our active years, and a comfortable old age when we're too old to work.

It is quite clear that great changes in our economic and industrial life have forced government to intervene more intimately in our daily lives than was the case a century ago. Great concentrations of labor in large cities have become absolutely dependent for the necessaries of life upon continuity of employment; great farming regions have become dependent upon the products of industry and upon the continued purchasing ability of our urban centers. Neither group, nor any of the individuals in it, is capable of producing a livelihood out of its own efforts alone. Government cannot ignore the grave consequences of general unemployment; it cannot permit the economic stability of the nation to be subject to the capricious whim of a few men—no matter who they may be. Each of us depends for his daily sustenance upon the efficient operation of communication networks, of railroads, airplanes. In other words, man is no longer largely self-dependent.

The conditions of our life make us interdependent, and this circumstance has encouraged all of those who naturally lean toward paternalism in government to insist that only through collectivism, with centralized control of all our affairs, can justice, equity, and efficiency be maintained.

You and I agree that this type of thinking is completely false. But we must also agree that it has an appeal, and that it can be made to appear quite logical, particularly in those times when our economic system undergoes a "recession." Moreover, the need for constant revision and adaptation in methods and procedures encourages encroachment upon fundamentals.

At that point, Eisenhower heavily underscored the draft in ink. His forceful emphasis on the need for ceaseless vigilance against governmental usurpations or distortions of individual responsibility flowed directly out of his even more forceful insistence that the American system, as dynamic and flexible as the human individuals comprising it, must never become a sacred wall around a changeless status quo.

There are all shades and varieties of this encroachment upon the foundations of our system. Part of the attack is deliberately made, probably by people who hope to rise to positions of power on the doctrine of collectivism or statism. Such persons have no regard whatsoever for the good of the country, but their attack can easily be detected and countered unless we go completely asleep. But there are other individuals who are essentially humanitarian and altruistic in purpose even though they are fuzzy-minded in their thinking. They believe themselves to be "liberals," and in many instances they work unceasingly and devotedly in the promotion of ideas which, if adopted in our country, would merely advance us one more step toward total socialism, just beyond which lies total dictatorship. The problem of our day and time is how to distinguish between all those things that government must now do in order to perpetuate and maintain freedom for all—freedom from economic as well as political slavery—while, on the other hand, we combat remorselessly all those paternalistic and collectivistic ideas which, if adopted, will accomplish the gradual lessening of our individual rights and opportunities and finally the collapse of self-government. . . .

Here he harked back to his boyhood in Abilene and pride in doing a job well. Pride in work as the source of material and spiritual reward, he sometimes felt, was disappearing in the "attitude that the government owes us a living because we were born"—that we are to be rewarded without effort. Such corruption in the national attitude should be repudiated everywhere, he thought. Educational institutions had a particular responsibility.

Universities are great centers of research, of investigation, of free thinking. They are conventions of learned men, but to my mind they are meaningless unless they have underlying purposes that transcend mere discovery and imparting of knowledge. They cannot fulfill their mission if they concentrate their efforts only on the material betterment of their graduates. They must be aware of what the human soul craves, socially, politically, and economically.

In our case, at least, we find that individual freedom, all the basic rights of free speech, worship, self-government are the very core of all our deepest desires and aspirations. The universities must, therefore, point the way to perpetuation of these and be alert in warning us against all the insidious ways in which freedom can be lost. I do not mean to say that universities should be dogmatic, nor that they should be intolerant of opposition. On the contrary, I believe that they are all the better and the stronger for healthy argument, and, if our system is as correct in its basic principles and purposes, as you and I believe, it can well stand the most pitiless and searching examination—even by enemies. But if the things that we fear as threats to our venerated system are trends brought about by faulty leadership, by shallow thinking, and by sheer neglect, it seems to me that only through education, led by our great universities, are we going to get back on the right track.

My own belief is that Columbia University has a faculty capable of taking the lead in the study and analysis, from a national viewpoint, of these great social, political, and economic problems. . . .

It is in this light that I should like my friends to think of Columbia and of the work to which I am personally dedicated. In order to make progress, much is needed. Some of these needs are represented in more scholars and teachers. Another need is financial aid for outstanding students from all over the United States to come and meet with our great faculty. This means many more scholarships than we now have. Students must study in suitable surroundings, equipped with the necessary material things to make instruction effective. . . .

The moral and intellectual strength of Columbia is a great power for good in this country. Every year thousands of its graduates go back to their homes all over the nation. Thirty-five hundred of them go annually into the teaching profession. *To make sure that they are properly equipped, we need material things—money. This University could use, economically, effectively and immediately, at least fifty million dollars for necessary buildings and equipments, to say nothing of the large sums needed for endowment of teaching staffs. This is not to expand the University in numbers of students. That we do not want to do. We need the money only to give to the student we now have the best in education and understanding.*

Seldom has a college president been able to put so many of his personal convictions behind a fund-raising letter. But Eisenhower had grown increasingly aware of his convictions during the preceding years and, in any case, he felt that Columbia was worth all the effort he could give it. Despite his reluctance to solicit funds, he knew that without money there would soon cease to be a Columbia and that without it and hundreds of other similar institutions there would probably soon cease to be an America.

He worked tirelessly on Morningside Heights and while he had been able to do nothing about some of the building projects he had originally hoped to complete, he had at least contracted for a new field house for the athletic grounds—the first new Columbia building project since 1933. More important, he halted the trend toward a chronic annual deficit in the University's finances and revitalized the attitudes of the alumni and the public toward financial support of Columbia. Most important, however, so far as the freshman president was concerned, the University through its Teachers College had taken the lead in citizenship education.

With William Russell, President of Teachers College, he obtained from the Carnegie Corporation a grant of $450,000 for the purpose of teaching citizenship to students throughout the country and for the development of techniques in the field that would transform principles and precepts from fuzzily understood ideas into dynamic influences on everyday life.

"We can talk hours on end about those things," Eisenhower said to Russell, "about freedom and competitive system and the inescapable obligation that accompanies every right in our society, if any rights are to survive. But no matter how inspired and dedicated the speaker himself may be, or how brilliant his speech, the result may be nothing more than a flood of words. One concrete example can do far more good than a week of inspirational messages."

CHAPTER NINE

By January 1950, the citizenship education project was well under way at Teachers College. Educators from all over the country had sat in on discussions with Russell and Eisenhower. Within a few months, pilot courses had begun in eight school systems, and by March 1952 there were 400 participating systems with thousands of students in all parts of America.

But Eisenhower recognized that there was still one major area in which he had been able to accomplish nothing—the mobilization of the University's educational and intellectual resources in a continuing campaign to aid America to a better and sharper understanding of the problems facing the country.

"World revolution," he said, "of which one objective is the elimination of the American system of government, is the announced purpose of powerful forces. But this threat is no greater danger to the future of our mode of life than would be an accumulation of erroneous answers to currently perplexing questions." These he itemized, speaking to Columbia students.

"How can we faithfully pursue the ideal of world peace and friendship when, with discouraging frequency, we see rejected and scorned proposals that seem to us logical, just, and fair? How shall we, in international affairs, assume a firm and unmistakable position in support of freedom and American principles, but without giving to any person a fair basis for the charge that we are truculent or provocative? How shall

we maintain the costly military establishments necessary to international stability, yet avoid such stupendous national expenditures that they may dangerously bleed the economy? How can we carry out necessary programs of rearming potential allies and still avoid fostering the false and dangerous belief that armed might alone can guarantee peaceful security? How shall we protect the nation against insidious and even traitorous corruption in responsible places without endangering or reducing individual freedom or the civil rights of any individual? How shall we escape the unbalanced national budget with its inflationary effects and consequent damage to the wages, savings, and security of the average man, and do this without neglecting any of the national functions that are essential to the country's safety and the health of our economy? How shall we preserve as the constitutional purpose of government the welfare of all our citizens, but without making those citizens, or any significant part of them, unnecessarily dependent on governmental subsidy or subject to regimentation? Confronted by an ever increasing economic interdependence among all parts of our society, how are we to chart a sane middle course in the conduct of our affairs that will preserve to the individual the fullest measure of freedom and opportunity—to the nation, prosperity and strength and unity?"

Tentatively, and almost hesitantly, he broached the subject on August 1949 before the Columbia University Club of Denver. He spoke of the University's faculty as a sort of supreme court before which could appear a spokesman for every group or party that proposed an answer to any of these questions. The faculty would sit in judgment on the conflicting views. But such an arrangement soon proved to be impractical. He never referred to it again in just these terms.

During the fall, however, in speeches in New York City, and particularly before the Herald Tribune Forum, he clarified his thinking and arrived at the idea of an assembly in which men of all walks and backgrounds, gathered together in an atmosphere free from telephones and workaday pressures, might examine the major problems, work out some common ground, and arrive at operating conclusions. In November, his friend W. Averell Harriman, together with his brother Roland Harriman, whose imagination had been captured by Eisenhower's proposal, offered a site for the undertaking—Arden House, the family estate, on a 1300-foot wooded ridge, an hour's drive from New York City. Eisenhower visited the property on December 30, 1949, and examined the house itself, a mansion of great drawing rooms and endless corridors. He was immediately enthusiastic.

From then on, the American Assembly, as the project was shortly to be named, preoccupied Eisenhower's working time. Within a few months he had secured initial working capital of more than $500,000 from corporations, unions, foundations, and individuals. An additional $250,000 was raised to underwrite assemblies on various subjects. By early spring of 1950 Eisenhower was optimistic about his and the

University's future. Speaking in McMillan Academic Theater on the evening of March 23, he said:

"We hope to build here on the campus a Nutrition Center in which the world's scientists will find concentrated all the knowledge, the tools, the facilities that will enable them to devise better, more productive, and more effective techniques for the use of physical resources and the satisfaction of man's physical needs. We already have—and in every recent term we have further amplified—an Institute of International Affairs, where we hope the political and social leaders of the world will find concentrated the materials, the information, the masses of data that will enable them to adjust the stresses and needs of one area to the strains and surpluses of another.

"We hope to establish here a Chair for Peace, possibly an Institute. The purpose will be to study war as a tragic social phenomenon—its origins, its conduct, its impact, and particularly its disastrous consequences upon man's spiritual, intellectual, and material progress. All this we should study in a scholarly atmosphere, free from emotional bias and the daily crises of public life. No American university, I am told, has ever undertaken this comprehensive task. For me, there is something almost shocking in the realization that, though many millions have been voluntarily donated for research in cancer of the individual body, nothing similar has been done with respect to the most malignant cancer of the world body—war.

"We are presently engaged in a study of the Conservation

of Human Resources—restricted, as of now, to the United States—but which will be of immeasurable benefit to all the world in furthering the dignity of man as a human being. Another hope is to conduct an exhaustive study into the ways and means of applying to every man's good, in today's intricate economy, all the resources of America, in such a way as to maintain and enlarge every freedom that the individual has enjoyed under our system. There are other projects, under way or under discussion, that will take their places beside or even in front of these. Each of them will help Columbia University a little better to fulfill its purpose—the peace, freedom and good of America, and, therefore, of humanity."

Thus in three paragraphs, Eisenhower summed up the Columbia record to date. To make realities out of hopes would occupy the rest of his working days on the campus. And at the end of 1950, every project started by Eisenhower was on the threshold of success. But also at the year's end he received the call from President Truman, summoning him once again to Supreme Command.

CHAPTER TEN

IN THE LATE SUMMER of 1950, the American people lived on a daily diet of alarms, fears, and suspicions, aroused by the continuing threat of Communist expansion. Eisenhower, along with most of his countrymen, knew that despite the West's desire for peace, armed hostilities were just around the corner unless the free world acted quickly in its own defense; it needed a unified European army that would carry out the spirit of the Atlantic Pact. There were an increasing number of rumors that Eisenhower would be chosen to lead such an army. If he were chosen, there was no doubt in his mind that he would accept. Time and again he had insisted upon the need for European unity and the extent to which America's own defense depended upon it. There were many Americans, as well as a good number of Europeans, who disagreed, and among them was one of Eisenhower's closest friends. A letter from him arrived on November 1, 1950, nearly two months before President Truman called upon the General to go overseas, and within a few minutes Eisenhower, following a habit of long standing, had framed a reply:

. . . as to conclusions concerning my future responsibility and duty, I think you know my ideas on this perfectly well. Moreover, the longer I live the more I realize that no individual can predict with confidence anything concerning tomorrow. At this moment I am confronted with possibilities of profound import; possibilities that had not even crossed my mind as much as a month ago. You yourself mention them in your handwritten note. . . . You say, "I do hope that this week end you won't be talked into that Atlantic Pact job."

I am a little astonished at your use of the expression, "talked into." As you know, I am an officer on the active list, on which I will always stay, by reason of a special Act of Congress, affecting a few of us, unless I voluntarily remove myself from it. It is clear that my official superiors don't have to do any talking if they actually want me to take any military assignment.

But over and above such consideration and addressing myself to the merits of the case, I would conclude from your statement that you do not attach the same importance to the success of the Atlantic Defense Pact as I do. I rather look upon this effort as about the last remaining chance for the survival of Western civilization. Our efforts in the United Nations have been defeated by the vetoes of hostile groups—but in the Atlantic Pact we are not plagued by the hostile groups and are simply trying to work out a way that free countries may band together to protect themselves. If we allow the whole plan to fizzle out into a miserable failure, it would seem to me that our future would be bleak indeed.

Of course, if the authorities can find anyone else who will tackle the job, and who they believe can perform it, then I hasten to agree with you that that man would probably do it far better than I could. Moreover, I believe, in my present job, I am supporting an effort that will be of unusual significance to the welfare of our people. But I still would not agree that there is any job in the world today that is more important than getting Atlantic Union defensive forces and arrangements off to a good, practical and speedy start.

. . . all this may be meaningless; I do not want or need any other job. Moreover, I understand from the morning's paper that the Council in Washington seems further than ever from agreement. But the matter still retains its grave importance and so long as it does, any one of us—no matter what his station, his position or what personal sacrifices might be involved—must be ready to do his best.

Eisenhower had made a firm decision in the light of what he felt his duty to be and when the President telephoned, asking him to accept Supreme Command of the NATO forces, he was ready to take it. The call came late on the night of December 18, 1950. Eisenhower had spent the day at Heidelberg College, near Bucyrus, Ohio, where he had spoken to the students on his way out to Denver for the holidays. His thoughts that day were far from war and so was the subject on which he chose to speak.

"Whenever I get across the Alleghenies and start a westward trek," he said, "I feel that I am coming home. I was reared on the Great Plains of the Mississippi Valley and I recall once when I was in West Point—you know, the place is crowded in among hills—not knowing what was really the matter with me, I said, 'I wish I could get out of here to the plains again; I want to see somewhere.' My companion quipped, 'Yes, you want to go out to those plains, where you can see farther and see less than anywhere else in the world.' 'That is exactly what I want,' I said, 'some place where horizons are not limited.' "

But home for him was still a long way off. When he returned to his railroad car that had been standing on a siding, the call from Washington was awaiting him in a near-by freight house.

Eighteen days later, on January 6, 1951, General of the Army Dwight D. Eisenhower, Supreme Allied Commander, Europe, boarded a plane in Washington that was usually assigned to General of the Army George C. Marshall and flew to Paris. There and in the other Western European countries, he was to spend the following weeks studying the political, economic, and military elements in the defense situation.

That done, he would make his recommendations on the American course to the President and Congress. His trip began at the close of a black week.

No year since 1863, when a demoralized and bloodily whipped Union Army lay before Fredericksburg, awaiting the Mud March of one day and three miles toward Richmond —not even 1942—had opened for the American people under so gloomy a pall of military defeat as 1951. On the first day of the year, the New York *Herald Tribune* announced in a two-line banner head across the front page:

REDS OPEN ALL-OUT TWO-WAY DRIVE ON SEOUL:
BIG FORCE PUSHES ALLIES BACK AT TWO POINTS

And the next day in a three-line, four-column head:

SEOUL'S DEFENDERS DRIVEN BACK
THIRD OF WAY FROM 38TH PARALLEL
BY OVERWHELMING RED ATTACKS

On the third, the measure of military disaster grew more apparent with another, two-line, eight-column banner:

REDS OPEN GAP, ARE NINE MILES FROM SEOUL,
EIGHTH ARMY FALLING BACK ALL ALONG LINE

By Sunday, January 7, the newspaper's maps of the Korean situation no longer showed a front line. Everywhere the U.N. troops were falling back. The news was all of strong points abandoned; Communist advances and flanking drives; the enemy's van sixty miles below the 38th parallel and his troops in the outskirts of Wonju, pivot point of the U.N. defenses.

On the face of the news, it seemed that this retreat—the second in six weeks—might not end until the Americans and their U.N. allies were pushed back inside the Pusan perimeter. And yet, despite the cost in American lives and prestige, the Korean campaign was only a sector in a lesser flank of the Communist wars—hot and cold.

The main and central front was Western Europe, where small clusters of Allied troops—widely separated over a thousand-mile front—huddled together before Russian masses, estimated in the millions. On January 6, as the retreat in Korea continued, Eisenhower left Washington to undertake the organization of that main front. But as yet he was a supreme commander without an army. Behind him were ten crowded days, crammed with the rush of things that had to be done as one phase of his career ended and another began. For one thing, he had taken a morning out to rewrite his will in longhand, without benefit of counsel or legal advice, scrawling away at it in the penthouse of the Columbia president's residence, scratching out phrases, inserting lengthy clauses that wound between lines, down the margin, across the foot of the page, and up the other side, underscoring and amending until he had filled three pages that were indisputably an authentic Eisenhower holograph and very probably undecipherable by any probate court. But he had discharged to his satisfaction the obligation dinned into the ears of corporals and generals alike by the Adjutant General, that a will be made or brought up to date before the soldier departs for overseas.

Then, too, there were lengthy meetings with Columbia trustees, administrative officers, and faculty members; an academic enterprise with two hundred million dollars in assets does not lose a leader abruptly without feeling the shock. And in Washington, there were conferences with political and military leaders.

By January 7 there lay ahead of him a series of ordeals—physical, mental, and emotional; trial by air and weather and a split-second schedule. He was to undertake a grand tour of the West, from the Mediterranean to the Arctic, from beyond the Rhine to the Ottawa River in Canada, in order to estimate the needs and resources of the North Atlantic Treaty armies.

As bluntly as he could put his wishes, the Supreme Commander had forbidden any formal welcomes, parades, or staged spectacles with the keys to the city and speeches—plums in a pudding of uniforms and national costumes. The business of this trip was the security and defense of the West, the peace of Europe and the Western world. Demonstrations, requiring the expenditure of time and official attention, could be left to the Communists. Before it was over, the staff accompanying him—and they probably averaged twenty years his juniors, alert young men, used to the rigors both of field and desk—had been sidetracked in hospitals or were desperately hanging on to the ropes.

The tour ended Saturday, January 27, at Stewart Field, near West Point, minutes ahead of an ice and snow storm, the temperature nearing zero, visibility and ceiling almost nil. Photographic evidence of Eisenhower's return was a front-page picture in the nation's press, presenting the Supreme Commander and Mamie, their faces all smiles, their arms bulging with two grandchildren in snow suits.

The Eisenhowers moved into a suite at the Thayer Hotel at West Point, where for three days the General worked on his notes and reports. The following Thursday, he appeared before senators and representatives in the Library of Congress, and for ninety minutes, speaking extemporaneously, discussed the defense of the West against Communistic aggression. The next evening, by radio and television, he talked to the nation.

"As a soldier," he began, "I have been given an Allied assignment that directly concerns the security of the free world, with special reference to the countries bordering upon the North Atlantic Ocean. I have approached the task, aiming at the good of the United States of America, conscious that a strong, solvent America is the indispensable foundation for a free world. While I have reached certain conclusions, the subject of the free world's security is so vast and complex that no man could hope to master its elements to the last critical item or, in a quarter hour, to answer all questions to his fellow-citizens' minds.

"Our hope," he continued, "remains the achievement of peace based on understanding and forbearance, the only sure foundation for peace. We must never lose faith that such a peace can be ultimately established. We seek such a peace, and no one can honestly interpret our current modest preparations otherwise. . . . we strive to erect a wall of security for the free world, behind which free institutions can live. That wall must be maintained until Communistic imperialism dies of its own inherent evils."

After reviewing reports of Europe's inability and unwillingness to fight off aggression, he said: "That is a story often told. If it were the whole story, then all I could honestly do would be to recommend that we abandon the NATO treaty and—by ourselves—attempt, however futilely, to build a separate fortress against threatening aggression. Two striking facts make such a recommendation, for me, impossible.

"The first fact is: The utter hopelessness of the alternative requires our participation in European defense. We can all understand that America must be strong in air and sea power. These elements are vitally essential to the defense of the free world, and it is through them that we protect the approaches to our homeland and the routes of commerce necessary to our existence.

"But this alone is not enough. Our ships will not long sail the seas, nor our planes fly the world airways, if we stand aside in fancied security while an aggressive imperialism sweeps over areas of the earth with which our own future is inseparably linked.

"The second fact," he went on, "bearing upon our participation in European defense is that the people of Europe are not spiritually bankrupt, despite the validity of many pessimistic reports. Great sections of its population have for years labored on and fought the creeping paralysis of Communism. Now, the North Atlantic Treaty has brought new fuel to the flames of hope in Europe. It has noticeably lifted morale, the fundamental element in this whole situation—the force which powers all human progress."

He summed up his own personal position in three points. "To you, the people of America, I repeat—as I have to the Congress and to the President—I believe that:

"First, the preservation of free America requires our participation in the defense of Western Europe.

"Second, success is attainable. Given unity in spirit and action, the job can be done.

"Third, while the transfer to Europe of American military units is essential, our major and special contribution should be in the field of munitions and equipment.

"I shall go about my own task in this undertaking," he assured his unseen audience, "with the unshakable confidence that America will respond fully when the basic issues are understood. We know that one hundred and fifty million united Americans constitute the greatest temporal force that has ever existed on God's earth. If we join in a common understanding of our country's role today and wholeheartedly devote ourselves to its discharge, the year 1951 may be recorded in our history in letters as bright as is written the year 1776."

Meanwhile, he continued to examine his attitudes toward European defense and on February 28, a week to the day after his return to Europe, he wrote a long letter to a friend in Chicago, as much for the purpose of clarifying his own attitude for himself as for the elucidation of his friend.

CHAPTER TEN

Just before I left New York, I sent to you a very short letter in an attempt to lay before you the basis of my thinking with respect to our current international problems. While I have had no reply, I am now expanding somewhat on the same theme for a reason that I think to be valid.

Firstly, I want, fundamentally, to test my own conclusions against such as you have formed. This is because of my respect for the clarity of your thinking. If there should be a difference between us, I would certainly be most appreciative if you would point out to me any point where you think that I have gone astray.

Secondly: I have heard rumors that a number of individuals look upon my acceptance of military duty as a "joining of the Administration" and that, as a result, I not only participate in its policy-making, but I support all its foreign programs, possibly even, its domestic ones.

Of course, you personally understand that my performance of military duty bears no such implication whatsoever—you are quite well aware of the extreme degree in which I differ with some of our governmental foreign and domestic policies of the past years. So, I do not need to expound upon that phase of the question. But on the other hand, I thought it might be a good thing to have in your hands some exposition of my convictions with regard to our national security problem so that, from time to time, you would be in a position—if you find any validity in my line of reasoning—to help achieve that unity of basic purpose that we must have if this effort is ever to enjoy any success.

The nation's security problem is not as simple a black-and-white matter as the "Great Debaters" would like to make it appear. There is only one angle from which to approach any international problems; from that of "America first." I realize that argument cannot be presented in terms of slogans and catchwords but, because we have always attempted to classify people into conveniently labeled groups, I want to make clear that I am not *one of the "Internationalists" in the sense that I am willing to trust America's welfare to an international Congress of any kind.*

We, as Americans, face a deadly danger for a very simple reason. Communism, both ruthless in purpose and insidious as to method, is using the traditional Imperialistic designs of Russia and the present physical strength of Asia and Eastern Europe to promote the Communistic objective of world revolution and subsequent domination of all the earth *by the Communistic Party, centering in Moscow.*

My own adult life has been given over to the study of questions involving America's security and of serving in uniformed capacities in our security forces. During the latter part of this service, this Communistic danger has been steadily rising and has now reached a peak where definite, prompt, and comprehensive measures are necessary if we are to survive. Our position as the chief exponent of the free system—of the dignity of the individual and of a capitalistic economy—not only makes us the chief target of Communistic destructive purpose, but makes it incumbent upon us to be a bit wiser and more determined in our defense of freedom than would be the case in a country where devotion to these free principles does not burn so brightly.

Up to this point, I think there is no loyal American today who would disagree; the sole point of difference seems to be as to how *we should go about the task we understand must be performed.*

First and foremost, it is almost trite to say that our own country must remain solvent; that bankruptcy for us would be a tremendous, if not decisive, victory for the Kremlin. One of the things Communism tries to prove to the peoples of the earth is that our system is weak, inefficient, and unfair. I violently disagree with any plan or program that ignores this basic principle, either explicitly or implicitly. I am sure that one thing worse than bankruptcy would be military defeat, yet it is my contention that the only way we can achieve military success either in preventing war or in winning a war is through preserving the integrity of our economy and our financial structure. *This means courage in facing up to sacrifice—both individual and national.*

Communism acts both through threat of aggression by means of armed force and by internal subversion, bribery, and corruption. This combined effort has been so long sustained against Western Europe that this region is by no means the healthy, strong, and virile portion of the world that we considered it back in the days of 1914 or indeed in 1934. Yet the importance of Europe to America's security is not by any means to be minimized.

On the purely military side, the transfer, by force or by

subversion, to Communistic control of the great industrial complex of Western Europe, including its tremendous numbers in skilled labor, would be for us a major catastrophe. If the Eurasian Continent were one solid mass of Communist-dominated people and industry, there would be no possible military dispositions on our part that could protect the Continent of Africa except possibly its southern areas. Among other areas, the Belgian Congo, the Mid-East, and the Suez Canal would be gone!

The military strength of such a Communistic combination, organized and armed under Communist dictatorship, would be staggering; and the existence of such a vast organism, hostile to us, would pose a military problem that would defy solution. Aggravating the whole situation would be the fact that over and beyond this would be the economic problem. Where would we get the materials needed for our existence? For making steel, for making atomic bombs? It is this kind of possibility that keeps me awake nights, keeps me pondering as to applicable policy, and keeps me working in a position and in a region that I had fervently hoped and prayed would forever belong to my past. Nothing else could have moved me to the personal and family sacrifices entailed. So, as far as personal inclination is involved, this kind of thinking and concern for my country completely defeats my former hope of devoting the remainder of my years to constructive aims. I thoroughly believe that, at Columbia University, I was contributing something toward the future safety and health of the American form of democracy.

CHAPTER TEN

If all the eventualities I have presented on the world situation are only reasonably accurate, it is clear that American efforts to rejuvenate in Europe a feeling of self-respect, of self-confidence, and of self-dependence—including the burning purpose and desire of self-defense—are not only worthwhile, they are mandatory because of the utter bleakness of the alternative. I have no means of knowing just how efficiently the Marshall Plan has been administered nor exactly how effective it has been in restoring economic capacity and in helping revive the spirit of Europe. The testimony here is to the effect that without the Marshall Plan, Europe would already be under the control of Moscow. In any event, the present question is how to inspire Europe to produce for itself those armed forces that, in the long run, must provide the only means by which Europe can be defended. *Over the years, I agree that there is no defense for Western Europe that depends conclusively or even materially upon the existence in Europe of strong American units. The spirit must be here and the strength must be produced here. We cannot be a modern Rome guarding the far frontiers with our legions if for no other reason than because these are* not, *politically,* our *frontiers. What we must do is to assist these people to regain their confidence and get on their own military feet.*

The American material *effort, I think, could and should be limited as to* length of time; *I consider it an error to try to predict and fix its limits, as of this moment, in terms of exact degree of effort. While I do not know the length of time that some occupational troops may be in Germany, I would say this: If in ten years, all American troops stationed in Europe for national defense purposes have not been returned to the United States, then this whole project will have failed.*

There is no use exploring the various directions in which the international situation could have, in the meantime, been drifting, but it is quite certain that should Europe as a whole fail, in ten years and with our help, to rebuild the economic, military, *and* internal *strength required to preserve itself inviolate against Communism and Communistic attack—then the United States will have no recourse but to seek some other solution to this desperate problem. But, in the meantime, the issues are so great, the contrast between what could be won and what would, through neglect, be lost is so all-embracing, that I do not believe we should place, in advance, announced size limitations upon our effort. These would tend to retard or discourage the rebuilding of European spirit, which must be the foundation for European strength.*

I repeat that there is no reason whatsoever for writing this letter except my respect for your ideas and convictions; and the thought that you may find occasional opportunity to help clarify thinking on these vital matters.

The NATO setup was highly complicated, plagued from the start with many of the same sort of problems that had wrecked the Philippines Defense Plan. Firm leadership was absolutely essential in order to circumvent the inevitable delays arising from traditional European nationalism as well as from the hostility that many Americans maintained in the presence of a United States alliance with the Continent. Eisenhower would have to depend upon his talent for military leadership as well as his gift for statesmanship in greater measure than ever before. The Russian armies, poised along the West's tenuous frontier, were a continuing menace, but a more serious threat was the West's own reluctance to band its forces together for mutual defense. There were many factors to be considered in achieving unity and Eisenhower had alluded to them often during the preceding years.

In his final report as Chief of Staff, in 1948, he said:

The order of battle is now a vast array of men and machines, extremely fluid; operated in three dimensions, whose spearhead and sources of supply, even though thousands of miles apart, are joined by a continuous pipeline. Political, economic and social forces, as well as strategic and tactical, influence its organization and operation.

To direct an enterprise as complex as the combined NATO forces requires that its leaders understand more than mere strategy and tactics. They must have a firm grasp of a thousand and one variables involving not only the military structure of any given country, but its economic, social, and cultural components as well. They must know the industrial potential of each nation and the dependability of its labor supply and be able to anticipate the staying power of its average citizen in the event of hostilities. They must be able to determine how much of its resources—natural as well as financial—each country can contribute to the joint effort and to what extent its traditional values are likely to prevent it from joining a co-operative enterprise involving all the other Atlantic Pact countries. In other words, the leaders of an international defense force must be armed in military doctrine.

The Russians, on the other hand, seem to conceive of successful warfare simply in terms of mobile masses of men, heavily armed, and impelled by fear and fanaticism. No one can doubt the stamina and bravery of the individual Russian soldier, the tactical ability of his generals, or the efficiency of his weapons.

Should the Russians move against the West this year, the advantage in man power immediately available will almost certainly be theirs. Very likely they will outnumber the West in planes, artillery, and armor. Possibly, they may be on equal terms in atomic weapons. But in the decisive element the Russians will be disastrously inferior. That element is military doctrine.

By this index of military might, the West seems to be invincible—if it can achieve unity, and through unity gain maximum effectiveness in the use of its men and materials. Russian man power and the man power of her satellites, including Asia's hordes, would be powerless despite their superiority in numbers to overcome a well-knit Western defense line—a defense line strengthened by its leaders' awareness of the political, social, economic, and industrial factors, as well as the purely military ones, which combine to make the modern army fully effective.

CHAPTER TEN

Through the spring and summer months of 1951 Eisenhower met many people who questioned him on the imminence of war. His answer on one occasion was:

Suppose you and a dozen of your friends constituted the Politburo within the Kremlin. You control all decision of war and peace for the Soviet masses. At home, you are entrenched in power; within the Russian borders there is no threat you need fear, no group that can despoil you of your dignities, your luxury apartments, your automobiles and planes, your retinue of servants. Within the last few years you have seized, beyond the Russian frontier, an industrial and agricultural empire whose complete absorption will strengthen you at home and abroad and increase even further the wealth you enjoy. Your hold there, however, is not yet secure. Millions in Poland and eastern Germany and Czechoslovakia and Hungary and the Balkans accept your bondage in sullen silence, awaiting the first moment when they can lunge desperately at you and your supporters.

So situated, will you risk your position and your future against the Allied armies and navies and air fleets, whose present stature is only a faint index to their overwhelming might should the nations that now muster them be resolved into a cold-blooded and avenging unity by your attack? I think I can answer the question for you.

So situated, you—of course—would hesitate at the irrevocable decision of war. You might hope that your armies could cross the Elbe and some of your divisions might probe forward to the Rhine. But the Channel and the Bay of Biscay and the Western Mediterranean would be beyond your grasp.

As your armies faltered before the Allied wall; as units from the satellite countries mutinied, deserted, straggled away, your lines of supply and communication would be destroyed by air attack; your own cities would be battered; the Black Sea might easily become an Allied lake.

To the woods and morasses of Poland would throng patriots, armed by air, commanded by parachute-dropped leaders, able and eager to purge their land of everything Russian. The Balt and Czech and Hungarian towns and villages would rally guerilla forces to harry you. Unrest at home would follow, and each day your power, your prestige, would shrink. In that light—confronted by a stout Allied line, before you and on your flanks—you, or a Russian, would hesitate at going to war deliberately.

Despite this optimism, Eisenhower planned to take no chances. He began his campaign for unity from the day of his return to Europe, February 21, 1951, when he and his wife along with members of his staff and their families moved into the Trianon Palace Hotel in Versailles to await the move to permanent homes at Marnes-la-Coquette. Throughout the rest of the winter and into the spring and summer, one of the Supreme Commander's major responsibilities was to learn the shape and readiness of every unit under his command. Before the summer was over he had personally inspected every substantial land, sea, and air unit from Norway to the

Mediterranean. His inspections were frequently arduous, but he enjoyed them. They were a relief from his office chores and they offered him much the same sort of chance to get into the field with troops that he had wanted back in Fort Lewis.

The Italian Alpine inspection was typical:

At 2:30, on the afternoon of April 24, 1951, he tossed the last staff paper into the out-going basket on his desk, placed his cap on his head, walked down the Astoria Hotel's grand staircase, and climbed into his car for Orly Airport. Air-borne at 3:00, he landed near Udine on the Italian side of the Alps at 5:30. A half dozen generals were awaiting him with a cavalcade of cars. He was surprised to see uniforms, for he had expected no formalities, then grinned, shook hands all around, and took off for the villa where he was to lodge during his stay. Cocktails with the generals, dinner with his own staff of four, a walk through the garden, a bull session around the fireplace, early to bed—it was a nice leisurely evening, like the quiet hush before the cyclone rips.

He was up at dawn, gulped his coffee, and the inspection tour was under way. The first stop was the defense works along the Tagliamento, forty miles away. There the Supreme Commander left his car, crossed several ditches, climbed a hillside, walked through some tunnels, and checked the lines of fire, asking questions of staff officers who followed along after him. It was 8:30 when he climbed back in the car and headed for the passes through the Julian Alps.

He rode as high as his car could go. The temperature dropped; the road grew steeper. At a level spot where parking was possible, the party transferred to jeeps; Eisenhower's leading a winding procession along a road that snaked between overhanging rocks, curled around shelves in precipitous cliffs, wound up and beyond the snow line to a trail that only pack mules and mountaineers could climb. On foot, Eisenhower climbed another six hundred feet vertically, a mile and a half as the path zigged and zagged across treacherous snow banks and boulder-strewn shoulders, to the observation platform where he was to watch the Giulia Alpini Brigade maneuver against an invading force from the East. It was then 9:45.

For two hours he watched the Alpine troops through field glasses as they skied at breakneck speed down the slopes, swarmed over vertical cliffs on dangling ropes, and pushed demolition and bazooka squads forward under cover of pack artillery fire. The valleys and precipices reverberated to mortars, machine guns, and rifles; the echoes volleyed across the frontier into Austria and Yugoslavia, a few miles away. Clad in parka and fur-lined boots, the Supreme Commander stamped from end to end of the platform for a better view. As he studied the contour map during lulls in the firing, he gulped black coffee against the cold and asked questions about the numbers and disposition of units, their training program, average length of service, morale; sometimes nodding with pleasure, as the interpreter gave him an encouraging answer; sometimes urging a change in program or suggesting a new experiment in tactics, watching hawk-eyed the Alpini officer's face for his reaction as the interpreter turned Kansas American into Tuscan Italian. A provident planner had set out chairs so that the spectators could watch the two-hour exercise. But Eisenhower chose to stand; there were too many things to see, too many questions to ask. With the last strong point overrun, the last fortification demolished, he turned to the Italian officers, anxiously awaiting his judgment.

"A wonderful show," he exclaimed, as the staff broke into grins. "I never saw anything like it before. Excellent. Well done. Those Alpine lads are as tough and hardy as I've seen anywhere!" It was then 11:48.

He led the returning spectators down the mountainside, plunging at near-Alpini speed over the snow that grew more treacherous as it softened under the noon sun. Once in their jeeps, the party returned to a lower valley for lunch in the Alpini barracks.

When lunch was over, some of the troops asked the General to come outside and inspect the men whom he had not been able to see during the exercise. He agreed and walked out only to find himself encircled by a group of the Alpini, who wanted to make him an honorary member of the brigade and present him with the feathered cap, symbolic of the mountain men. He accepted, was photographed, and told them that he would always proudly treasure the feather, evidence of his comradeship with a splendid fighting unit. Then he, and the interpreter, walked through the ranks, talking to the men: "Where are you from? What did you do before you came into the army? What will you do when you get out? How do you like your outfit? Do they feed you well?" The men glowed with pleasure; here was a new sort of general.

It was then 1:30. The party moved back into the automobiles and after a wild ride across the plain, during which they stopped hastily to review a mule pack battalion, they were on the maneuver grounds for the Mantua infantry division exercises before 3:00.

A platform and tent had been erected on a hillock. There again, the Supreme Commander watched the troops parry and then rout an invading thrust. Artillery shells, from guns in close support, roared overhead. The observation tent was in the direct line of fire. Staff officers worried that one faulty shell might wipe out the Italian General Staff and the Supreme Commander as well, but Eisenhower—who knew the possibilities as well as they—continued stomping across the platform, moving far forward to get a better view of the exercises. Almost on the dot of 5:00, the maneuver was over.

There were a few squads of soldiers that had particularly attracted the Supreme Commander's attention, and he wanted to talk to them. He spent a few minutes with one corporal in particular, who had handled his squad on the field with veteran precision. The boy—he was hardly twenty—had been drafted twelve months before and next week he was to go home to his farm near Naples, his service ended. "Don't you like the army?" Eisenhower asked. "Yes, sir." "Why don't you stay in?" "Well, I am proud to do my duty, but now that

I can, I would rather go home." "I know just how you feel," laughed the General, clapping the corporal on the shoulder.

Once more, the party entered the cars; they returned to the villa, where they changed and cleaned up before driving on to Udine for a regimental dinner with the 76th Napoli Infantry Regiment. After the ceremonial meal and long discussions with senior Italian officers about the day's exercises, there followed a visit to the noncommissioned officers' club, where there was more talk about the exercises, this time on the sergeant and corporal level; next a tour—the Supreme Commander protesting that he was invading the men's privacy—of the enlisted barracks, the mess halls and kitchens, the recreation rooms; and, finally, the return trip to the villa. Eisenhower had been on the go since six in the morning; and he would be up the following morning at the same hour.

Thursday, April 26, opened with more coffee and more fast driving down narrow and winding lanes. Suddenly they halted at a main road. The corporal from Naples was waiting with his squad. The previous evening they had learned the route the General would be traveling, got permission to leave their barracks before daylight, and here they were to ask him: "Will you accept the honorary leadership of our squad?" He would and they formally decorated him with the red-and-white foulard insignia of the unit. "I'm glad to have this as my own squad," the General told them when the ceremony was ended. Then he asked each soldier to write his name in the memo book that he pulled out of his pocket, and he passed his fountain pen around. "I want to keep a record of this," he told them.

He resumed his drive, stopping at the barracks of three units along the road to the level plain outside Beano, where the tanks of the Ariete armored brigade were lined up for inspection.

Half of Italy's armored force was there, a single line of World War II surplus tanks, discarded by the United States Army. The tanks gleamed. Their battle scars had been painted over. Broken and damaged plates and treads had been replaced by handmade parts. The crews stood sharply at attention. Evidently hours upon countless hours had been put in by the men so that the Supreme Commander would be impressed by the care they took of their American equipment. But there was no evidence, as Eisenhower trudged the line, that any of the vehicles had moved under their own power in weeks.

"Order the men to move their tanks forward fifty yards," he told an Italian officer as he passed the last tank. Observers held their breaths, awaiting the test. Orders were shouted, men clambered into place, motors sputtered into a deafening roar. A few minutes' pause for warm-up, then from left to right in a parade line the tanks moved forward in unbroken front, crossed ditches, hummocks, and holes, and continued on a good two hundred yards to halt in a line almost as perfect as the inspection formation.

Black wrath creasing his forehead, his eyes ablaze, the Supreme Commander descended on the officer to whom he had given the command. "Did you order those men to advance fifty yards as I told you?" he demanded through an interpreter.

The officer, shaken by Eisenhower's lightning conversion from calm to fury, stumbled badly while the Supreme Commander—patient again—waited for him to gather his wits. Haltingly, he began his explanation. He had measured with his eye a distance of fifty yards, he explained, and had seen that the ground was very badly broken there. If the tanks halted there, he continued, some would be tilted forward, some backward, presenting nothing like the front the Ariete should present to their Supreme Commander. Repressing a smile, Eisenhower—the interpreter translating almost simultaneously—delivered a lecture on strict obedience to a superior's commands. That done, he saluted the troops and was off again.

Next on the schedule was a review of the Bersaglieri. When he reached their barracks, the General mounted an observation platform in the inner courtyard and for forty-five minutes watched thousands of men put on a spectacular exhibition of gymnastics, infantry drill and regimental review at double time. Even the band came on at a run, instruments playing; falling into formation, the men continued to play without muffing a note. Never before had he seen anything of the sort and, through the entire spectacle, he had hardly a word to say as he stared at the troops trotting before him.

"I have never been so impressed in all my life," he told the Bersaglieri officers when the exercise was ended. "If these troops are not victorious on any battlefield, it can only be because of overwhelming odds against them." Once again he was presented with an honorary membership in the unit and a plumed Bersaglieri helmet. As the group returned to the automobile convoy, he continued to repeat his astonishment at the performance and stamina of the troops he had just seen. One member of the party, however, muttered to another: "Me? I am just as much impressed by what *he* has been doing to *us* since yesterday morning."

Although such inspection trips as these were exhausting, they were a pleasant departure from the more discouraging aspects of his work, such as the countless disputes involving personal prestige and national sovereignty. But Eisenhower had grown used to such squabbles and knew how to take them in his stride, and by late June there were several tangible indications that he had begun to weld the separate contributions of ten nations into a single team. Supreme Headquarters remained a kaleidoscope of uniforms—flaming reds and sky blues, Scottish tartans and American O.D.s. But the initial babel of tongues, thanks to compulsory classes in English and French, the two official languages, was soon reduced to a murmur. And the spirit of unity was evident daily in the dining room, where the four chairs around each table were usually occupied by men and women of four nations.

Yet, however much Eisenhower and his staff may have accomplished in building morale and laying the groundwork for continued co-operation, the defense effort also depended upon the response of Western Europe and America to calls for arms and money. America, Eisenhower knew, would meet its commitments—even though belatedly—but Europe was a different matter. Each country presented unique difficulties.

Late in June, Eisenhower decided to attack the problem directly. In a speech delivered in London before the English-Speaking Union, which was attended by Attlee and Churchill along with a thousand others, he discussed Europe's situation point by point.

In his opening words he referred obliquely to a growing rift between the Americans and British over naval command in the Atlantic. "This unity of ours [America and Britain] in fundamentals," he said, "is an international fact. Yet on more than one occasion, it has been obscured in Britain and in my own country by concern with trifles and small disputes, fanned into the flames of senseless antagonisms.

"Serious differences in conviction," he continued, "must be beaten out on the anvil of logic and justice. But scarcely need they be dragged into the public forum, in the petty hope of capturing a fleeting local acclaim, at the expense of an absent partner! There are men in this room with whom, in World War II, I had arguments, hotly sustained and of long duration. Had all these been headlined in the press of our two countries, they could have created public bitterness, confusing our peoples in the midst of our joint effort. Decisions were reached without such calamitous results, because those at odds did not find it necessary to seek justification for their personal views in a public hue and cry.

"Incidentally," he added smilingly, "a more personal reason

for this expression of satisfaction is a later conclusion that my own position in the arguments was not always right. In any case, may we never forget that our common devotion to deep human values and our mutual trust are the bedrock of our joint strength."

Then, after talking for a few minutes about the united front against aggression throughout the world and particularly in Korea, he plunged into his topic.

"It is a truism that where, among partners, strength is demanded in its fullness, unity is the first requisite," he said. "Without unity, the effort becomes less powerful in application, less decisive in result. This fact has special application in Europe. It would be difficult indeed to overstate the benefits, in these years of stress and tension, that would accrue to NATO if the free nations of Europe were truly a unit.

"But in that vital region, history, custom, language, and prejudice have combined to hamper integration. Progress has been and is hobbled by a web of customs barriers interlaced with bilateral agreements, multilateral cartels, local shortages, and economic monstrosities. How tragic! Free men, facing the specter of political bondage, are crippled by artificial bonds that they themselves have forged, and they alone can loosen! Here is a task to challenge the efforts of the wisest statesmen, the best economists, the most brilliant diplomats . . ."

He went on: "Europe cannot attain the towering material stature possible to its peoples' skills and spirit so long as it is divided by patchwork territorial fences. They foster localized instead of common interest. They pyramid every cost with middlemen, tariffs, taxes, and overheads. Barred, absolutely, are the efficient division of labor and resources and the easy flow of trade. In the political field, these barriers promote distrust and suspicion. They serve vested interests at the expense of peoples and prevent truly concerted action for Europe's own and obvious good."

These were harsh words, indeed. Eisenhower, in them, struck at all the national pride, customs, and traditions of a continent. But the reward to Europe, he believed, warranted his outspoken temerity.

"With unity achieved," he continued, "Europe could build adequate security and, at the same time, continue the march of human betterment that has characterized Western civilization. . . . It would mean early independence of aid from America . . . The coffers, mines, and factories of that continent are not inexhaustible. Dependence upon them must be minimized by the maximum in co-operative effort. The establishment of a workable European federation would go far to create confidence among people everywhere that Europe was doing its full and vital share in giving this co-operation.

"Any soldier contemplating this problem would be moved to express an opinion that it cannot be attacked successfully by slow infiltration, but only by direct and decisive assault, with all available means.

"The project faces the deadly danger of procrastination,

timid measures, slow steps, and cautious stages. Granted that the bars of tradition and habit are numerous and stout, the greatest bars to this, as to any human enterprise, lie in the minds of men themselves. The negative is always the easy side, since it holds that nothing should be done. The negative is happy in lethargy; contemplating, almost with complacent satisfaction, the difficulties of any other course. But difficulties are often of such slight substance that they fade into nothing at the first sign of success. If obstacles are of greater consequence, they can always be overcome when they *must* be overcome. And which of these obstacles could be so important as peace, security, and prosperity for Europe's populations? Could we not help? We, the peoples of the British Commonwealth and of the United States, have profited by unity at home. If, with our moral and material assistance, the free European nations could attain a similar integration, our friends would be strengthened, our own economies improved, and the laborious NATO machinery of mutual defense vastly simplified."

In delivering this speech, Eisenhower called upon the whole store of his fundamental American convictions concerning co-operation and the need, in times of danger, to submit self-interest to the good of the community.

He did not call for the abolition of national boundaries or the annihilation of proper self-interest among the countries of Europe, but he urged in the most forceful terms he could muster that neither boundaries nor self-interest should impede mutual defense. There was danger in the world for solitary nations. And by the time Eisenhower had finished his address, most of those nations knew it.

Their response, as indicated in the press during the following days, was heartening. Eisenhower, so it seemed, had done more for European unity in ten minutes than a host of statesmen had been able to achieve in the previous five years.

The month of July following the London visit was relatively free from pressures. The Supreme Commander had more leisure for a full family life than at any other time in several years. With the Eisenhowers were their son John and his wife Barbara, their two children David and Ann, and Mrs. Eisenhower's mother. The family spent many happy days together, and Eisenhower was delighted to be with his grandchildren. The quiet interlude ended on July 28, when the younger Eisenhowers, their leave nearly over, returned to the United States for West Point and John's new assignment to Fort Knox. With them went Mrs. Doud.

Thereafter, the routine reasserted itself. On July 24, the Supreme Headquarters had been moved from Paris to suburban Marly. A month later, the Eisenhowers moved from their temporary quarters in the Trianon Palace Hotel to the villa at Marnes-la-Coquette, bought for the Supreme Commander by the French Government.

Through the early fall months the defense forces grew in numerical strength. Arms, however, remained a critical problem. The European industrial plant could not provide the necessary equipment. The sole hope was America and American aid. But the multiple civilian agencies of the American

Government, concerned with the European economies—ECA and ERP, MDAP, and others—were a maze of entanglements. Despite all the good will and co-operation in the world, there was bound to be delay and makeshift. Not until Eisenhower, recalled briefly to the United States by the President in November, made a direct and personal appeal to Washington authorities did the entanglements begin to straighten out. He won assurance that arms and supplies would be forthcoming. But he learned, on the other hand, that the American people were far more interested in his becoming President of the United States than his remaining in charge of European defense.

CHAPTER ELEVEN

ONCE MORE Eisenhower had become the subject of intense political speculation and again he made it clear that his duty, as he saw it, was not to seek high office. The European defense forces were developing smoothly but there were still plenty of obstacles ahead, not the least of which was the continuing, though at the moment somewhat diminished, threat of a Russian move. Accordingly, the sense of duty that had taken Eisenhower to Europe in the first place seemed likely to keep him there indefinitely.

But the pressure from home grew steadily greater during the fall of 1951 and Eisenhower found himself increasingly unable to ignore it. More and more he was obliged to analyze his own thinking on national politics—to define once and for all his convictions and responsibilities. Throughout his career he had never entertained any ambitions that did not accord with his sense of duty. But now the definition of duty no longer seemed as clear-cut to him as it had once been. Where exactly was his duty? In Europe, where the defense of the West and ultimately of America itself seemed to depend upon his remaining with SHAPE, or in America, where he had reason to believe the people wanted him for their president? His answer, he knew, would certainly constitute the most important decision he had ever made. He pondered his choice throughout the entire fall and into the winter; then finally on January 6, 1952, United States Senator Henry Cabot Lodge, Jr. announced that the General's name would be entered in the March 11 New Hampshire Republican primary. The senator confidently declared: "He will not withdraw. He is in the race to the finish," and added: "It is worth noting that in our conversations with General Eisenhower he pointed out that he would never seek public office but would consider a call to political service by the will of the party and the people to be the highest form of duty."

An Associated Press correspondent assumed that Lodge and his colleagues expected the General to ask for relief from his European defense command so that he could return to the presidency of Columbia University, possibly in February. Some Democrats doubted Senator Lodge's authority to speak for Eisenhower; they themselves planned to enter his name in the New Hampshire Democratic primary. The senator, however, insisted: "General Eisenhower has personally assured me he is a Republican."

The following day, at Supreme Headquarters in France, Eisenhower clarified his position in a formal statement:

Senator Lodge's announcement of yesterday as reported in the press gives an accurate account of the general tenor of my political convictions and of my Republican voting record. He was correct also in stating that I would not seek nomination to political office.

I have frequently and publicly expressed my refusal to do so.

My convictions in this regard have been reinforced by the character and importance of the duty with which I was charged more than a year ago by our country and the other nations of the North Atlantic Treaty Organization. America's enlightened self-interest and the future of Western civilization alike demand success in our collective effort to produce security against Communistic threat and to preserve peace.

Under no circumstances will I ask for relief from this assignment in order to seek nomination to political office and I shall not participate in the preconvention activities of others who may have such an intention with respect to me.

Of course there is no question of the right of American citizens to organize in pursuit of their common convictions. I realize that Senator Lodge and his associates are exercising this right in an attempt to place before me next July a duty that would transcend my present responsibility. In the ab-

sence, however, of a clear-cut call to political duty I shall continue to devote my full attention and energies to the performance of the vital task to which I am assigned.

Apparently, Eisenhower had come a long way since his letter to Leonard Finder in 1948. But actually his basic convictions had not changed in the least. Repeatedly in his speeches he has emphasized the obligation of every American to live up to the responsibilities that his citizenship imposed. Rights and freedom, he has said over and over again, cannot exist unless every individual enjoying them is prepared to sacrifice some of his personal inclinations on their behalf.

The logic of this argument, together with the nature of the present political situation, obliged Eisenhower to revise many of the attitudes he had held in 1948. His duty, as he saw it in the fall of 1951, was to obey any "clear-cut call" from the people of his country. Such a call would, he felt, "transcend [his] present responsibilities," and he would have no choice but to heed it. His feelings concerning high office echoed those of the late Chief Justice Charles Evans Hughes who once said: "The Presidency of the United States should be neither sought nor declined." Certainly this was no attitude to arouse the enthusiasm or win the support of professional politicians. Reluctance in a candidate, according to them, assures his defeat—as it seems to have assured Hughes's defeat.

At Supreme Headquarters he was in a position somewhat

similar to the one he had held ten years earlier in Fort Lewis while awaiting a call to assume a troop command of his own. When General Marshall finally ordered him to lead the Allied armies in Europe, he was ready to accept the challenge, but until Marshall called, he entertained no greater ambition than to fulfill his assigned responsibilities as long as they gave him the opportunity to employ his talents to the best of his ability. His present duties are at the disposition of the American people.

He is, by virtue of the climate in which he was raised as well as the convictions he has held all his life, a Republican. In all of his public statements dealing with political issues in either the narrow or broad sense, he has consistently expressed his belief in the value of independent action on the part of each private citizen, unhindered and unhelped by the federal government except in instances where government assistance is clearly needed.

In matters of government control, as on all other topics, he is, as he declared before the American Bar Association, in St. Louis during 1949, a middle-of-the-roader. He will accept social change when circumstances demand it but he abhors it when its seems unnecessary. He is far from being a reactionary—as is indicated, for example, when in 1950 he chose Henry George over Stonewall Jackson for a place in the Hall of Fame—but he refuses to accept the catch phrases and visionary schemes of social planners who hope to revise the existing social order by means of one or another proposed reform. Americans, he feels, do not need to be led by the nose in order to achieve a decent level of prosperity. If they are willing to work hard—and work together—then there should be enough for all those who deserve it.

For a friend who late in the winter of 1951 inquired what he thought a progressive's political philosophy should be, Eisenhower worked many evening hours writing the following letter:

Historically, the task of the progressive in human relationships has been, in essence, an unchanging one. It is to combat and break down concentrations of power, of whatever kind or location, whenever these unjustifiably or unnecessarily exercise authority over the lives and fortunes of men. Stated in another way, the real progressive is dedicated to the idea that there should be assured to every individual the greatest possible opportunities for self-development and advancement, spiritually, intellectually, economically. He should be protected against injustice and unnecessary domination, of whatever origin. This requires orderly government.

Human experience has demonstrated the need for numerous types of political, business, and social organizations. Since the basic purpose of all organization is to produce orderliness, which means restriction upon irresponsible human action, some control of the affected individuals is accepted as an essential factor in successful group functioning. National governments, local church organizations, school systems, boards of directors and labor unions are examples of organizations in which certain restrictions upon human be-

havior are enforced or implied, to the end that the common interests of all may be served.

It is difficult to define the exact line of demarcation between necessary control and rules of conduct on the one hand, and unjustifiable seizure of power on the other. But in political governments a practicable testing ground is found in a system of periodic, free elections participated in by all the individuals affected in the particular organization. Government by the consent of the governed is scarcely conceivable without the observance of this custom. In its absence centralized control tends to verge closer and closer to regimentation, as individuals wielding power become more and more intoxicated with its exciting experiences, and the people sink deeper into apathy or helplessness.

The American revolutionary leaders were progressives in the true sense of the word; they clearly saw that the control exercised by George III over the American colonists was unjust and unendurable. So they set about the business of destroying that control. Theodore Roosevelt was a progressive because he, convinced that great concentrations of wealth and industrial productivity were giving to a few men an excessive degree of influence over the happiness and livelihood of a nation's masses, set about the business of diminishing and diffusing that power.

Power concentrations can be local, as in a boss-ridden city, or almost limitless in scope, as in the case of the Roman Emperors. They can be basically political, which means all-inclusive in their influence over the people affected, as in the case of the Kremlin politburo. They can be largely financial in composition, within political organisms dedicated otherwise to personal liberty, as was the case in practically all industry of the Western World during portions of the nineteenth century.

As already noted, all men recognize the need for some control over their own impulsive actions; so that the exercise of individual freedom may not limit the freedom of others. The more complex the society, the greater the volume of such laws.

It is well to realize that many of these restrictive laws applying to business and to industries, now accepted as necessary to an orderly and a measurably free life, go into much broader fields than that of mere personal deportment or conduct. Witness our anti-trust laws, social security plans, minimum wage scales, interstate commerce regulations, and communications laws. Many of them have been passed by the votes of both parties and with large majorities. Over and beyond these, the country has welcomed in the past a host of laws enacted for the relief of economic distress and natural catastrophe; it is safe to say that no American Government of today would dare to stand idle if we should suddenly enter, again, a depression like unto that of 1932. On the contrary, the government would be expected to use the entire resources of the country to prevent disaster. The point is that this should be done without violation of our basic concepts of freedom, justice and right. But though conditions of the modern industrial world make mandatory types and kinds of governmental action that a century ago would have caused open rebellion, it is well to note that the very requirement for such laws makes it more than ever important that we resist unnecessary regulation, else the process will gain a momentum that could prove irresistible.

It is needful, also, to stand watch to see that new financial despotisms do not arise, even though they could scarcely come into existence except with the consent of, or because of the weakness of the over-all political organization. The conclusion is that weak government favors the predatory; too strong a government (dictatorship) regiments us all. In the mid-ground between the two extremes of complete laissez faire and governmental control is found that condition which best satisfies the aspirations of man as a spiritual and intellectual as well as a material being. To attain that mid-ground or practical balance is difficult, but it is the ever-continuing problem of free men.

In the United States, because of the circumstances of its founding and the great care exercised by the framers of the Constitution, there was little early *danger of dictatorial political power—but conditions so developed as to make the influence of concentrated wealth a menace to the self-respect, opportunities, and livelihood of great groups of ordinary citizens. The process of controlling, diminishing, and diffusing the power of concentrated wealth has been a long and gradual one, conducted on many fronts. Against abnormal concentrations of economic power we have arrayed, in the history of our country, both local and federal governments, the influence of church and school, and the pressure of organized labor bodies. The winning of that battle was essential to the maintenance of the individual. Nevertheless, the process itself has set up habits of thought, customs and practices that could become dangerous. Already, in some instances we are suffering from too much government—or unwise government. While the balance we seek is not easy to find or to preserve, yet it is not difficult to identify certain directions in which imbalance has become acute. These, as progressives, we must correct.*

Extravagance in governmental spending has brought about unbearable taxes—taxes which, if long continued, will strangle incentive, the very quality which built the nation. In spite of this the governmental debt rises. The government seems, at times, to resort to an interpretation of anti-monopoly laws that permits it practically to blackmail legitimate enterprise. It has so played upon and distorted the true meaning and intent of the interstate commerce responsibility that it attempts to arrogate to itself functions, even police functions, that specifically belong to the states. The government deserted the gold standard (whether necessary or not is now immaterial). The value of our money has become the football of politics—subjected to the political whim of the moment. Inflation has partially destroyed our savings and our life insurance values.

The government penetrates more and more into our daily living; its answer to excessive control is more control. In this whole process the abuse of the taxing power has been one of the chief weapons the government has used. It is a favorite weapon for three reasons. The first of these is that it is the readiest at hand. The second is that unjust and unwise taxation, tending toward the destruction of freedom, can be made to appear, temporarily, as humanitarian concern for the masses. Slogans like "Soak the rich" are sweet to the ears of millions, and the protests of the few who discern the catastrophic effects upon the worker and the freedom of the masses are scornfully dismissed as the screams of the wicked, enduring deserved punishment. The third reason is that few people are conscious of the connection between a prosperous free enterprise and freedom—national solvency and individual freedom. Worthless money and bankruptcy lead to nationalization of property; a development that compels bureaucratic control, which must finally give way to autocratic control.

So our problem is to preserve the opportunities of all citizens to make certain that our synthesis of social, economic and political organization and procedure is designed to bring happiness and prosperity to the millions, and, while doing this, to prevent unwarranted governmental encroachment into our private affairs—to examine the need for each of the alleged necessary controls over private business and living.

The framers of the Constitution considered the proper distribution and allocation of political power to be one of the most important of their tasks. They divided it functionally into three parts; the legislative, the executive, the judiciary.

So we have the Congress, the great offices headed by the President, and the judges. But the founding fathers felt it necessary also to divide and diffuse power geographically! Thus the states and the local governments. Constitutional provision states that all powers not specifically accorded to the Federal Government were reserved to the states respectively, or to the people. Note! The framers of the Constitution did not make the Federal Government the repository of any residual or unspecified powers or of functions that might later become necessary to exercise! They wisely provided for diffusion—they were wise men.

Now, consider the effect of excessive Federal taxes on local government; in examining the subject briefly, we must keep in mind the basic purpose of the Constitution's framers to avoid the danger of over-centralization of power.

In the original Constitution, the kinds of taxes that could be levied by the Federal Government were limited. Without enumerating here the avenues by which it was allowed to obtain revenue, it was necessary, in 1913, to amend the Constitution in order to apply the graduated income tax. Hardly anyone seriously questions the justice and fairness of a graduated income tax as part of our entire revenue-raising process, but the significant thing is that in adopting the amendment it was not felt necessary at that time to impose any constitutional limit as to amount or percentage of income that could legally be taken, or to specify the fields of taxation that should properly be reserved to the states. It was assumed that the good sense of our government and the watchfulness of our *people would take care of this. But thus the way was opened for a central majority to impinge upon constitutional provisions without appearing to do so.*

Our courts have stated that "The power to tax is the power to destroy." A corollary would seem to be: the power to tax is not only the power to destroy the individual business or the corporation—it could also spell the destruction of the several states. If the Federal Government uses its taxing power to the point that there is no money left to the citizen for payment of taxes to his city and state—these local agencies of the people will become helpless—possibly even disappear. . . .

We reach the clear conclusion that in those instances where circumstances appear to force governmental intervention into citizens' affairs, we should try, earnestly try, to assign the duty to a local echelon of government. There is a vast difference between one of the several states supporting an activity and the Federal Government performing the same function. There is, firstly, the certainty that local citizens will keep a closer watch over expenditures for any kind of purpose when paid for exclusively by them than when the funds seem to come freely from a far-off Washington. Secondly, and far more important, the local government cannot debase our currency in order to pay its bills. A Federal deficit is blithely incurred because of power to make a new issue of bonds or currency—thus hurting the standard of living of every citizen in the country. Under this threat, each of the several states is almost compelled to seek Federal grants in order that it may gain some material return for the losses forced upon it. The process is insidious—if at first it seems painless its results can nevertheless be catastrophic.

Possibly, the false prophets of bureaucratic control are no longer so influential as once they were. But danger still exists. It is found in peacetime budgetary deficits, in stifling Federal taxes, in the piling up of governmental debt. Our money grows cheaper and cheaper; and the only cure that the "planner" offers is more of the same, "Give me more power, let me, whether in peace or war, control prices of materials and of labor, let me control imports and exports, let me control production and sales, let me issue more money, let me allocate and apportion to each what I see fit to allocate and, I promise you (says the hardened bureaucrat) all will be well!" And the victim is not the wealthy man—one who could possibly, in any case, live out his days, if he so chooses, in idle comfort. It is the workman, the mass of America, that is to pay the price; regimented labor is the inescapable basis of the socialized or planned economy!

For this development, so far as it has gone, possibly each of us has to shoulder a bit of responsibility—we've liked the soporofic effect of paternalism and wishfully hoped that somehow harvests would grow without planting; and, even if not, then that all of us might be fed without harvests.

No one challenges the need of central controls in times of government crisis—in fact, we demand them! But when they remain with us indefinitely, the citizens should beware!

Every man who looks these things in the face, every man

who dares to challenge the assertion that bureaucratic government must not replace constitutional forms, which still hardily persist, must be prepared to hear the screaming charge of reaction, of selfishness, of favoring the vested interests. He must be prepared to hear himself labeled an economic Tory, who fails utterly to place men above money, decency above profits. Such foul and lying tactics are as old as history—but they can be effective. The demagogue played his part in the destruction of Athens and of Rome.

On the other hand, the same individual who is labeled by the radical theorists as a reactionary will often be himself called a radical by the extreme reactionaries. We have men who will not admit any need for, or justice in, the graduated income tax or any excuse for such fact-finding and semi-judicial bodies as the Interstate Commerce Commission, the Security Exchange Commission, and so on.

The true progressive must refer again and again to the axiom that liberty is not possible for one except as it is defined and limited by equal liberties for others.

Thus, we would have nothing but chaos if an individual radio station was not compelled to observe the rules and regulations laid down by a central body of recognized authority. The need for anti-trust laws was found in the habit of concentrated wealth to eliminate all competition and then gain a relatively abjective power over the lives of citizens, limited only by the need for the product or service supplied by the resulting monopoly. These and many similar examples can be cited by any high school graduate to show that prog-

ress can be achieved only in the middle-ground, the center of the road between these two doctrinaire extremes.

Even though many voters later sought to learn his position on certain specific and controversial matters, circumstances hardly permit him to provide the sort of answers they want. Not a professional politician, he had neither the time nor the staff to set forth publicly to every voter the convictions which he maintains—and has maintained for years—on foreign and domestic matters. Defense of the West occupies all his time as well as the time of those around him. Furthermore, he has a stout repugnance toward indicating outspoken partisan activity so long as he has remained a soldier in the service of all Americans whatever their political affiliations. He has, after all, set down his general convictions in speech after speech, and to a friend who wrote him recently concerning his political platform, he answered:

To a certain extent, the record of every individual (at least any classed as a public figure) is a thing for all to read. What candidates might promise in specific cases in order to win a nomination—assuming that they are ambitious in this regard—and what their whole lives may have exemplified could conceivably be entirely different things. As of now, based upon the information I gain from letters written by my friends, I feel safe in saying that the great concern of the American people is for: (1) renewed assurance that we really have a two-party system; (2) honesty and integrity in government; (3) acknowledgment that the resources of even such a country as ours have limits; (4) that reckless and excessive spending and taxation can, in the long run, be as dangerous to our way of life as are external threats; (5) hope of establishing an administration in Washington that can provide a unifying influence, possibly even inspiration; (6) a hope of getting an administration characterized throughout by a sense of justice, fair play, and consideration for all our citizens rather than slickness in appealing to special interests and pressure groups; and (7) confidence that our affairs in the outside world will be handled intelligently and firmly so as to regain for us a position of security and respect, and to do this in such a way as to avoid extravagance. Such ideas can be expressed in numerous ways, and the groupings I have given could be better stated.

They could, of course, be increased. In the past I've given my views, emphatically, on all of them, time and again, so I must assume that you have in mind something far more concrete and specific.

In view of his responsibilities, he could not be more concrete and specific. This much is certain, however. Any decision he makes that concerns America will stem directly from his basic convictions concerning America's place in the world and the strength of her average citizen to uphold that place.

Freedom, dignity, and responsibility are not catch words with him. He shuns the hollow sound of demagoguery and upholds the firm belief that the future of America depends upon the opportunity of every man to demonstrate his worth in free competition with all others. Therein is the foundation on which his political convictions rest. The remainder is contained in the substantial body of his public statements which repeatedly emphasize the simple faith that has sustained him from Abilene to Paris and which has served, in the face of countless obstacles, to unify the free world against its common enemies and which will, he is convinced, continue to do so as long as mankind upholds individual dignity over the power of the state.

On the evening of March 23, 1950, he addressed an audience at Columbia, and in his talk summed up the basis of his personal philosophy. He said:

"As citizens of the United States, you and I—and all Americans in every corner of our land—must be forever mindful that the heritage of America and the strength of America are expressed in three fundamental principles: First, that individual freedom is our most precious possession; Second, that all our freedoms are a single bundle, all must be secure if any is to be preserved; Third, that freedom to compete and readiness to co-operate make our system the most productive on earth. Only within the framework of these principles can we hope to continue the growth that has marked our history. Only thus can our millions reach the fullness of intellectual, moral, and physical welfare that is justly ours—and avoid any risk of submission to the all-powerful state. Moreover,

only thus can the world have any hope of reaching the millennium of world peace—for without the example of strength, prosperity, and progress in a free America, there is nothing to inspire men to victory in today's struggle between freedom and totalitarianism.

"As friends of free people everywhere in the world, we can by our own example—our conduct in every crisis, real or counterfeit; our resistance to propaganda and passion; our readiness to seek adjustment and compromise of difference—we can by our own example ceaselessly expand understanding among the nations. We must never forget that international friendship is achieved through rumors ignored, propaganda challenged and exposed; through patient loyalty to those who have proved themselves worthy of it; through help freely given, where help is needed and merited. In this sense there is no great, no humble among us. In rights and in opportunity, in loyalty and in responsibility to ideals, we are and must remain equal. Peace is more the product of our day-to-day living than of a spectacular program, intermittently executed.

"The best foreign policy is to live our daily lives in honesty, decency, and integrity; at home, making our own land a more fitting habitation for free men; and, abroad, joining with those of like mind and heart, to make of the world a place where all men can dwell in peace. Neither palsied by fear nor duped by dreams but strong in the rightness of our purpose, we can then place our case and cause before the bar of world opinion—history's final arbiter between nations."

Neither before nor since has he offered a clearer statement of his own position. It is not in his nature to promise the free people of this country—or of any other—anything that they themselves cannot achieve by their own co-operative efforts. It has always been his habit to delegate responsibility where it should properly reside. And the responsibility of free citizenship resides with the people.

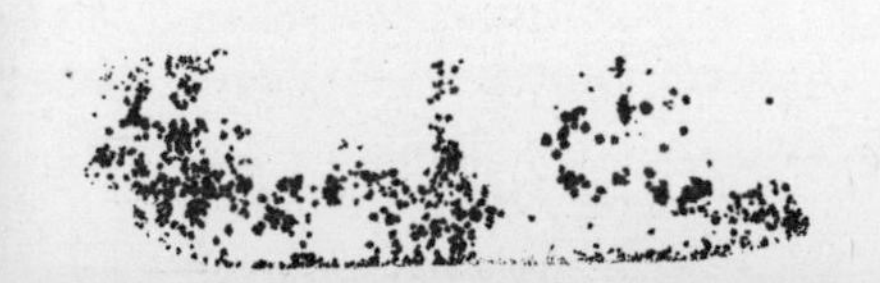

① Abilene, Kansas, to 1911. ② West Point, New York, to 1915.
③ Mexican Border and Texas Training, 1915-17 and 1941.
④ Camp Colt, Gettysburg; Fort Dix; Camp Meade, Maryland, 1918-
⑤ Panama Canal Zone, 1922-25. ⑥ Leavenworth C & G S School, 1925-2
⑦ Washington, D. C., 1927, 1929-35.
⑧ Paris, France, 1928-29. ⑨ Manila, Philippine Islands, 1935-3